SPRINT

ALSO BY JAKE KNAPP AND JOHN ZERATSKY

Make Time: How to Focus on What Matters Every Day

Sprint: How to Solve Big Problems and Test New Ideas in Just Five Days (with Braden Kowitz)

CLICK

How to Make What People Want

A Proven System from the World's Most Successful Startups

Jake Knapp

with John Zeratsky

AVID READER PRESS

New York Amsterdam/Antwerp London Toronto Sydney/Melbourne New Delhi

AVID READER PRESS
An Imprint of Simon & Schuster, LLC
1230 Avenue of the Americas
New York, NY 10020

First Avid Reader Press hardcover edition April 2025

AVID READER PRESS and colophon are trademarks of Simon & Schuster, LLC

Interior design by Ruth Lee-Mui

Manufactured in the United States of America

1 3 5 7 9 10 8 6 4 2

Library of Congress Cataloging-in-Publication Data has been applied for.

ISBN 978-1-6680-7211-0
ISBN 978-1-6680-7213-4 (ebook)

This book is for the founders, leaders, and teams who

inspired and taught us along the way.

And you. Yeah, you. This is for you and your team, too.

Contents

Preface

I run inside Orcas Island High School just as the late bell sounds, stumble on the threshold, and drop my three-ring binder. Sheets of paper explode across the linoleum floor. Panting, face hot with embarrassment, I scoop up the pages. I pat my coat pocket. The disk is still there.

Now, upstairs. Down the hall. First door on the left. I peek through the window, then give the handle a slow turn. The computer lab is empty except for one kid: my friend Ian.

"Dude," Ian says. He's spending his free period playing solitaire, stacking cards on the screen, his eyes glazed.

"I've got a new game," I say. I bring out the floppy disk I've carried from home and hand it to him.

It's 1993, I'm fifteen years old, and the software on the disk is not just any old video game. It's homemade. I've spent the past year, including my entire summer vacation, building this game, writing the code and drawing the artwork pixel by pixel. I wanted to keep it a secret until it was ready, and today? It's ready. I'm excited. But I need an opinion from someone I can trust. Someone brutally honest. Someone like Ian.

He arches an eyebrow and takes the disk. Then the door bangs open and our friend Matt barges into the computer lab.

"What's this?" he says, joining Ian beside the computer.

"Some new game," Ian says as he begins to play. I stand back, silent and nervous, and watch.

The game is your typical swords-and-sorcery castle adventure. Ian figures out the controls and begins moving from room to room. His character finds a torch and then a dagger and then . . .

"Eh," Ian says. He scoots back and looks at Matt. "Want a turn?"

Wait, what? Something's wrong. Ian's character hasn't died. He hasn't even fought a monster yet. The Ian I know would never willingly hand over the keyboard midgame, unless . . . I wince. *Unless the game is boring.*

Matt takes over. And yeah, something is off. He's not leaning forward. He's not talking trash. This is not the Matt I know. When a giant spider kills his character, Matt does *not* start over to seek revenge. Instead he stands, stretches, and says, "You guys wanna shoot some hoops before our free period is over?"

"Let's do it," Ian says.

Damn it. They're choosing *exercise* over a video game? My stomach sinks. *All that work. How could I have been so stupid?*

This book is about what I learned that day: Turning a big idea into a product that people love is *really* difficult. Getting it wrong can be a *colossal* waste of time and energy. Getting it wrong hurts.

But there is a reliable way of getting it right. There is a system for making things that people love, and I first stumbled on it back in high school—although it took me decades to recognize it.

After Ian and Matt shrugged off my castle adventure game, I was bummed. Still, I didn't want to give up.

I realized it wasn't enough to just make a game—if I wanted people to actually *play* the game, it had to beat out the alternatives. During free period, that meant my game had to be more fun than solitaire—which seemed doable. But my friends could also play basketball. They could listen to mixtapes on their Walkmans. They could walk to Island Market and buy a corn dog.

Basketball, Walkmans, corn dogs. Tough competition.

Now that I knew what I was up against, I went back to work, only this time, I ran experiments.

Every week or so, I would take just the beginning of a new game—a prototype—to school and show it to my friends. I tried space quests, strategy battles, sports games, you name it. Every time, they shrugged.

Until I came up with a game I called "Mealy Mouse."

In Mealy Mouse, the player moved through a series of mazes. My friends didn't exactly love it at first, but I saw promise in their reactions. They leaned forward when they tried it. So I kept experimenting. I sped up the pace of the game. I added loud and humiliating sound effects that went off whenever the player made a mistake.

One day, I brought a floppy disk to school, handed it to Ian, and this time? He kept playing until Matt shoved him over. This time? Matt talked trash. This time? My friends Sean and Sean got in on it. This time? Even *girls* tried the game. Nirvana.

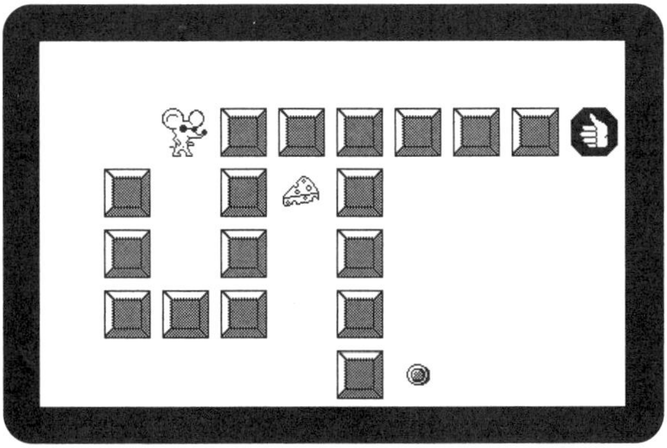

Then our math teacher, Mr. Fleck, walked into the computer lab. He asked what the hell we were doing, then he watched, and then . . . *he* asked for the next turn.

Me? I sat back and watched them play. I was so stoked, I felt a thousand feet tall. Because, for the first time, I made something that clicked.

Introduction

Every once in a while, a new way of doing things comes along and everything clicks. The new way solves an important problem. It's unique. People hear about it and it makes sense, so they try it, and when they do? It delivers. The new way is so good that it makes the old way look like junk.

But most new products don't click.

They flop.

So what's the difference? What makes one new product a runaway success? What makes another fail?

Of course, there are a zillion factors. Team. Management. Technology. Execution. Design. Pricing. Timing. Luck. But all of these lead (or don't) to one decisive question:

Does it click?

This is the most important thing. The product and the customer must fit together, like two LEGO bricks.

If a product solves an important problem, stands out from the competition, and makes sense to people, it clicks. If not, it's a dud. That's it. Making it click is the fundamental key to success.

I know, this is pretty obvious stuff. But even though it's the most important thing for any big project . . . it's kind of easy to lose track of the click. We get wrapped up in the technology and execution and design and pricing and all the other important factors—and in the noise, we forget the paramount question:

When we offer this to people, will they want it?

All too often, we bet on the wrong strategy, and our products don't click, they flop.

But it doesn't have to be like this. There is a better way. And that's what this book is all about.

This book is based on firsthand experience with some of the world's most successful startups.

Early in our careers, my coauthor, John Zeratsky (JZ), and I had the good fortune to build several successful products. JZ joined a startup that was acquired by Google, then became a leader on Google Ads and YouTube. I worked on Gmail and cofounded Google Meet. We know what it's like to start a big project and see it through till it clicks with customers. But what's special (and unusual) is what happened in the second half of our careers.

Since 2012, JZ and I have worked directly with early-stage startups, first as partners at Google Ventures and now as cofounders with Eli Blee-Goldman of the venture fund Character Capital. Most investors give advice, but when I say "work directly," I mean precisely that. For more than a decade, dozens of times each year, we've cleared our calendars—for a day, a week, or even a month at a time—to work side by side with founders and their teams in "sprints" to kick off their most ambitious projects.

JZ and I have run more than three hundred of these sprints. Along the way, we had a hand in smash hits like Flatiron Health, Gusto, One Medical, Blue Bottle Coffee, and Slack, among many others. Today we work alongside startups at the forefront of artificial intelligence. It's a unique opportunity and a ton of fun. I mean, who else in the world gets to join founders in these crucial moments, time and time again? We're like two kids with FastPasses at Disneyland.

But I have to admit that our motivation for working this way is partly selfish: our money is on the line. We run sprints with founders because it's the best way to make their products click with customers, help their companies succeed, and lead to a positive return on our investment. These sprints are serious business.

The first type of sprint I created was the Design Sprint, which I developed based on methods I used at Gmail and Google Meet. JZ and I refined the Design Sprint at Google Ventures, then wrote a book about it called *Sprint.* The book became a bestseller, people around the world adopted the Design Sprint, and to this day, we hear stories about teams running these sprints at companies like Airbnb, Amazon, Apple, OpenAI, Tesla, and even LEGO. The success of the Design Sprint surprised us. I guess that's an understatement—we were blown away.

But after starting Character Capital, we noticed something was missing. Design Sprints are awesome for solving problems and testing ideas, but in the early days of a new company, founders need a different kind of help. They need a plan for standing out from the competition. And they need to choose a direction and get started—as fast as possible.

JZ and I wanted to help. We looked for patterns in the most successful projects we've seen firsthand as designers and investors. We realized these patterns could help *any* kind of big new project—not just startups. So we reverse-engineered those patterns into a new sprint format that we call the **Foundation Sprint**. We call it the Foundation Sprint because it creates the foundation on which a team can build a product that clicks.

Today, the Foundation Sprint is the tool we use most often with the companies in our portfolio. In this book, we'll give you the secret recipe.

This book is about unlocking the power of the fundamentals.

Teams who build winning products share some fundamental traits. They know their customers—and what problem they can solve for them. They know which approach to take—and why it's superior to the alternatives. They know what they're up against—and how to radically differentiate from the competition.

This combination of customer, approach, and differentiation forms what JZ and I call a Founding Hypothesis. The Founding Hypothesis distills a team's strategy into one *Mad Libs*-style sentence:

Founding Hypothesis

If we help	customer
solve	problem
with	approach
they will choose it over	competitors
because our solution is	differentiation

The Founding Hypothesis is simple, but that's exactly what makes it so powerful. Products click when they make a compelling promise—and that promise must be simple, or customers won't pay attention.

Every winning team JZ and I worked with made one of these simple, compelling promises. For example, when I worked on Gmail in the 2000s, our promise to customers was: "We'll solve your overflowing inbox problems better than Outlook, Hotmail, and Yahoo because we offer more storage and great search."

Gmail

Founding Hypothesis

If we help	tech enthusiasts
solve	overflowing inboxes
with	Google data center power
they will choose it over	Outlook, Hotmail, Yahoo
because our solution is	high-capacity & searchable

In our book *Sprint*, we profiled several startups who built products that clicked. Again, looking back, it's easy to identify the simple promise each one made to customers.

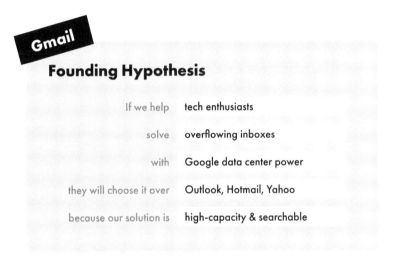

Here's how the Founding Hypothesis could have looked for Blue Bottle Coffee, a startup we worked with in 2012:

Blue Bottle Coffee

Founding Hypothesis

If we help	coffee drinkers
solve	need for a break
with	artisan coffee & chic cafés
they will choose it over	Starbucks
because our solution is	delicious & beautiful

For Flatiron Health, a startup we worked with in 2014:

Flatiron Health

Founding Hypothesis

If we help	cancer care clinics
solve	finding the best therapy
with	AI for clinical trials
they will choose it over	manual search for trials
because our solution is	fast & comprehensive

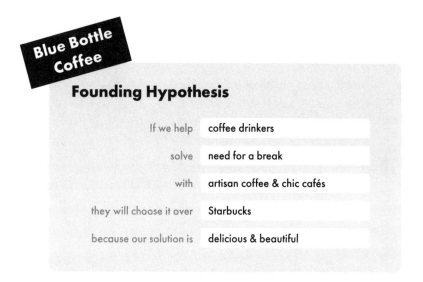

And for Slack, a startup we worked with in 2015:

Slack

Founding Hypothesis

If we help	**teams**
solve	**communication**
with	**searchable chat**
they will choose it over	**email**
because our solution is	**fun & boosts teamwork**

Each of these startups turned into a valuable business, and each was eventually acquired for hundreds of millions or even billions of dollars. In each case, they made a simple promise that clicked.

Unfortunately, finding the right simple promise is *not* easy.

When I first began working with startups, I was embarrassed to ask founders basic questions like "Who are your competitors?" or "How will you differentiate?" because I didn't want to waste their time or appear naive.

But once I worked up the courage, I learned a surprising thing: If I asked three cofounders to write down their startup's target customer, I got three different answers. If I asked a team what differentiated their product from the competition, I got a sixty-minute debate. The obvious stuff is not always so obvious.

And even if a team *does* have clarity about their promise, there is no guarantee that customers will care. For every Gmail, thousands of new projects at big companies fizzle. For every Blue Bottle Coffee, Flatiron Health, or Slack, millions of startups fail. Most teams can't find the right promise. They don't build what people want. There are just *so many ways* to get it wrong.

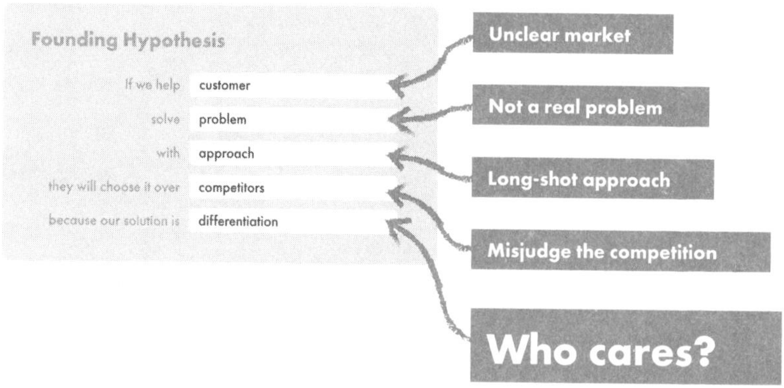

Why do so few teams get their foundation right?

Well, we're only human. Cognitive biases trip us up. Group dynamics are hard to navigate. People fall in love with their first ideas. Leaders don't know what's true vision and what's false assumption. They don't know how to run fast experiments. They don't know how to get the whole team committed and confident.

It doesn't help that the world's most popular approach to kicking off new projects is . . . chaos. Meet, and meet, and meet. Talk, and talk, and talk. Churn out slide decks, documents, and spreadsheets that no one actually reads. Outlast your opponents in a political cage match. Finally, rely on a hunch and commit to years of work.

That's the old way. And it is bonkers. Doing things the old way, it can take six months or more to develop a strategy. The old way is like assembling IKEA furniture by tossing parts, an Allen wrench, and a dozen squirrels into a broom closet, then hoping for the best.

There is a new way. You don't have to rely on luck: JZ and I have built, tested, and proven a system that will allow you to dodge cognitive biases, streamline group dynamics, make rapid decisions, and set up fast experiments. You can use the system to figure out what clicks.

• • •

This book compresses six months into ten hours.

Inside, JZ and I will show you how to create clarity on the fundamentals in just ten hours spread across two days.

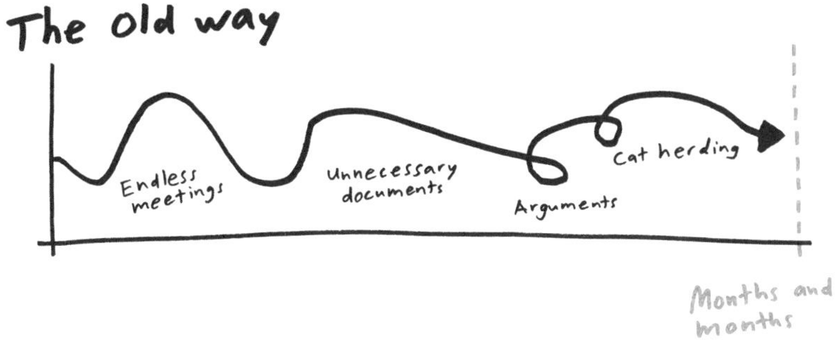

The Foundation Sprint works like this:

On day one, you'll focus on **basics** and **differentiation**. You'll identify the problem you're solving and form a plan to set your solution far apart from the competition.

On day two, you'll find the right **approach** for your project. You'll generate options, put them through rapid and rigorous evaluation, and choose one to try first.

At the end, you'll have your own **Founding Hypothesis**.

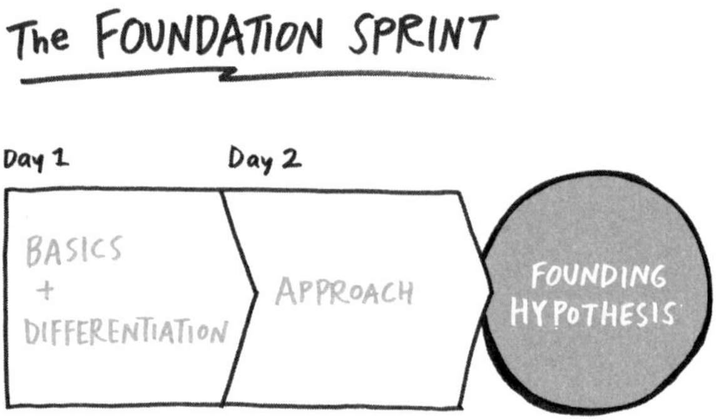

As its name suggests, the Founding Hypothesis is *testable*. By testing (and adjusting) your Founding Hypothesis up front, you can establish confidence that people want your solution *before* you spend loads of time and money building it.

So how do you run those experiments? With Design Sprints! If you've read our book *Sprint*, that's great. If not, we'll show you how to get started.

In the most ideal situation, JZ and I work with founders and their teams for four consecutive weeks. That way, they have time for a Foundation Sprint and three Design Sprints—which means they get multiple chances to create a solution that clicks with customers.

For big, ambitious projects, compressing so many tiny loops into such a short period of time is like fast-forwarding through years of product launches. You enter week one as a novice; you exit week four as a wizard of differentiation.

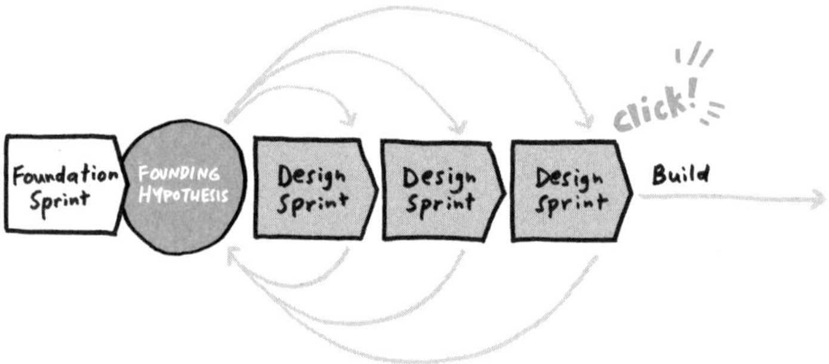

But I know that clearing your team's calendar can be a major challenge. Heck, depending on your organization, it might sound like swimming across the Pacific Ocean. Don't worry about that right now—the first step is simply reading this book.

This book is a great way to start.

Inside, you'll find ten brief chapters, each illustrating an essential lesson for defining the basics of your project (part 1), differentiating it from the competition (part 2), choosing the best approach (part 3), and using tiny loops to prove your strategy (part 4).

Ten chapters. Ten lessons. Personally, I find it hard to finish books that aren't written by Stephen King, and since I can't write like Stephen King, I made this book as short as I could. I also made it as useful as I could: I think you'll find that you can apply the lessons right away, even if you're in the middle of a project.

Then, when you're ready to run a full Foundation Sprint, you can use our checklist. It's at the end of the book, and it includes step-by-step instructions and a schedule. We also have an interactive guide with videos available online at theclickbook.com.

As an investor, I'm biased toward outcomes, and as a human, I'm biased toward meaning. I want projects to be both successful for their creators *and* valuable to the people they serve. That's why I'm super excited to share the Foundation Sprint with you.

In the Foundation Sprint, you create, as our cofounder Eli says, "the atomic building blocks of a great product." You craft an essential, just-what-you-need strategy at warp speed. Arguments disappear. Distractions evaporate. You can feel like a kid completely absorbed in an exciting project. You can also practice a new way of working with your colleagues, building great habits for today's ambitious effort and beyond. And you do all this with your customers—and what they want—at the center of your attention.

Trying a new way of working is a big investment in time and effort. It can be daunting, but you don't have to do it all at once. Here's a simple way to get started:

- Read this book
- Try some small pieces of the process with your team
- Next time you start a big project, clear your calendar, follow the checklist, and run a Foundation Sprint

You're still here? Great. It's not easy doing something new. But your customers are important, and you're doing this work for them. Let's get started.

Get Ready

Before the Foundation Sprint,

clear your calendar, gather your team,

and prepare for a new way of working together.

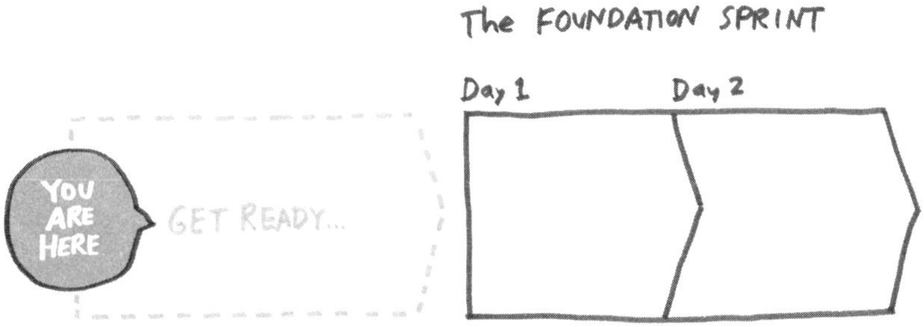
The FOUNDATION SPRINT
Day 1
Day 2
YOU ARE HERE
GET READY...

1

Reset

In January 2009, I took a weeklong business trip to Stockholm.

Now, before I say what I'm about to say, I want to state that I know Stockholm is a wonderful city. I know about the neat little islands, the enchanting architecture, and the lovely museums. I know they have terrific pastries. Some of my best friends are Swedes, so, for the record, I dig Stockholm.

But in January? It's kind of . . . miserable. It's cold. And dark. The sun barely rises and the sidewalks are piled with dirty slush.

And as I walked to the Google office in Stockholm, trudging through the miserable snow in the miserable dark on the first day of that business trip, I was miserable, too. I was about to meet with two brilliant colleagues and there was the possibility of a coffee and a pastry. But I was miserable because the three of us were working on a project that was about to die.

My friends were Serge Lachapelle, a French Canadian who had

lived in Sweden for years, and Mikael Drugge, a Swede from the far north of the country. We'd met a couple of years earlier, in 2007, when Google bought their startup. The three of us started talking about an idea for a new product: videoconferencing software that could run in a web browser. In those days, multi-way video calls were a hassle, so hardly anybody used them. We thought easy video calls could change the way people worked.

So we started a project to bring this new product to life. We compiled a giant slide deck. We wanted to come up with the perfect strategy to get the rest of the company excited. I became obsessed with the idea of a 3-D virtual conference room, and we added more and more ideas on top of it. Interactive documents and agendas and whiteboards and on and on . . . But our proposal was never *quite* perfect, so we just kept going and going and going.

Weeks went by. Months went by. A year and a half went by.

Then the global financial crisis hit. In January 2009, Google announced it was closing its offices in Trondheim, Norway, and Luleå, Sweden. I freaked out. I figured Stockholm was next, and if so, Serge and Mikael would be gone. And we still didn't have a coherent strategy. It was now or never. I booked a trip to Stockholm.

So there I was, in January, in the dark and the slush. I slogged down crooked streets until I found the Google office. I climbed the stairs of a drab gray building—*not* one of Stockholm's architectural highlights—and found Serge and Mikael waiting for me with big smiles and a cup of hot coffee. This felt like our last chance. But what should we do?

We decided to go a little crazy.

First, we set an audacious goal. It was Monday morning. By Friday, we agreed, we'd have a prototype of our software. Not a proposal, not a slide deck. A prototype. We would *show* everyone how great video calls in the browser could be.

Next, we decided on absolute focus. If we were going to create a prototype, we couldn't afford a single distraction. So we said "no" to every meeting on our calendars. We logged out of email and chat. We found a conference room with no windows.

Now, what should we build? Over the past two years, we had generated a few hundred ideas, but we couldn't design and prototype all of those in a week. So what was most important? It wasn't the 3-D virtual conference room, or the interactive meeting tools. No, the most important idea was simple: we wanted to create the easiest video-call software on the market. So that was what we would build—a prototype that made dead-simple multi-way video calls and nothing more.

We started working. We didn't have time to get things perfect, so we made quick decisions. We hashed out a design that was good enough. Then Mikael, an engineering genius, built the prototype. I remember the moment he got it working. He emailed me a link. I clicked and . . . boom. There was Mikael. There was Serge. Mikael said hello, Serge said hello, I said hello. We could see each other!

At the end of the week, we shared the prototype with other Googlers. It wasn't perfect, but people instantly understood the value. It clicked. Googlers started using our software for actual meetings; it spread across the company and eventually launched to the public. Today it's called Google Meet and has hundreds of millions of users.

I remember flying home from Stockholm and thinking, "Wow. That was different." For me, the most special aspect of the week wasn't *what* we accomplished, it was *how*.

During the year and a half before Stockholm, I treated the video-call project like any other project. Every week, I managed to spend a few hours on it, but I had to squeeze that effort in between other projects, meetings, and email. My focused hours were broken into tiny islands of time and scattered across the ocean of my workweek.

Before Stockholm

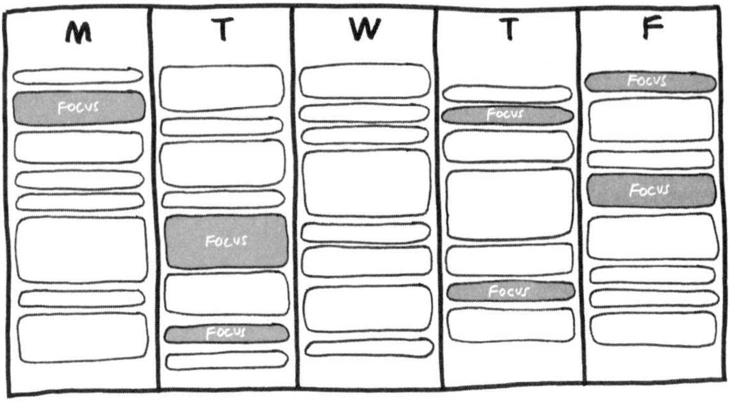

In Stockholm, we cleared our calendars and worked all day, every day, on the video-call project and nothing else. If the old way gave me islands of time, this was a continent. It was amazing!

In Stockholm

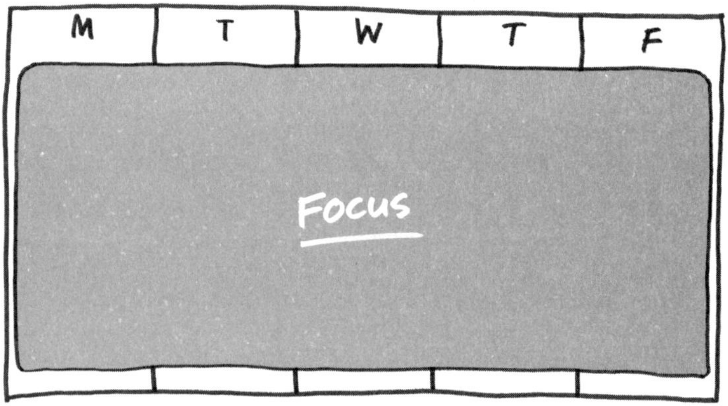

But it wasn't just *more* time, it was *higher-quality* time.

Before Stockholm, if I spent an hour on the project, I wasn't working for the entire hour. I might spend the first fifteen minutes getting my head into it, then fifteen minutes working, then I might check my email, and then it was time to think about the next meeting. If Serge, Mikael, and I got on a call for an hour, we'd spend half the time building context and half the time wrapping up.

In Stockholm, there were no context switches. Staying in context has a compounding benefit. The longer I worked on just one project, the deeper I could focus. Each night, my brain organized my thoughts as I slept. Each day, I became more focused and did better work.

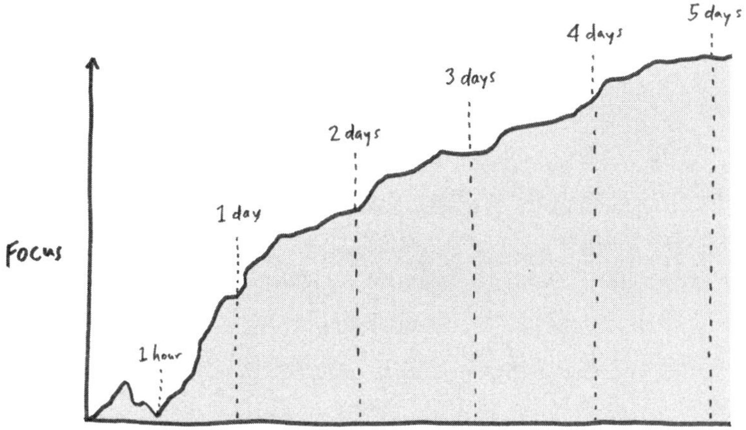

Source: Totally made up based on my experience, but it seems right, doesn't it?

There was also enough time for . . . *silence*. It wasn't a normal meeting or workshop atmosphere. We weren't constantly talking. Most of the time, we were thinking and working.

After that week in Stockholm, realization struck me—BANG!—like a two-by-four between the eyes. This didn't have to be a once-in-a-lifetime moment. Why couldn't all projects start this way? Why couldn't every team block distractions and focus on the most valuable core of their work?

That insight set me off on a quest to redesign how teams start projects, and I've been on that quest ever since. Here's the most fundamental lesson I learned along the way:

1. **Drop everything and sprint on the most important challenge until it's done.**

JZ and I have led sprints for hundreds of teams, and each time, we clear the calendar, focus on the most important challenge, and get it done. Every time, it works. My god, how it works! It's fantastic. It's almost supernatural. Clearing the calendar transforms what a team can accomplish.

But there is a small problem. This lesson—"Drop everything and sprint on the most important challenge until it's done"—is easy to say. But it's not easy to do.

In the modern workplace, we're supposed to attend meetings with teammates, managers, reports, business partners, and so on. We're supposed to stay on top of our email and messages. We're supposed to juggle multiple projects. And of course, we're supposed to meet deadlines and deliver results. That's a whole lot of "supposed to," and it makes it tough to spend a full uninterrupted day on one project—let alone two or five or fifteen days.

Unfortunately, working the way we're *supposed to* work means giving up the big win of building the best possible product in exchange for the small wins of obliging teammates on a moment-to-moment basis. Replying to emails and messages instantly? Going from meeting to meeting every thirty minutes? If we don't care about the big picture, then sure, go for it. We don't have to say no. We don't have to make tough decisions about our priorities. Everyone is happy . . . at least for today.

But if we think we can take on ambitious projects and make them click with customers while bouncing along through business as usual,

①

Drop everything &
sprint on the most
important challenge
until it's done.

ricocheting from one context to the next, we're fooling ourselves. Figuring out a project's strategy takes intense focus. Choosing the best opportunity among many options takes intense focus. Designing and building a prototype to test our hypothesis? Yup, that too requires intense focus. The normal way of working *does not allow for intense focus*—especially intense focus that is shared by multiple members of a team.

The solution is straightforward: make the difficult decision to call time-out, drop everything—all the constant email, constant meetings, constant context switching—and come together to focus on one important goal. Start your project with sprints.

Here are some techniques to help you drop everything, whether you're planning a Foundation Sprint or any focused burst of work:

Start with the Decider

The sprint team must include the boss: the person responsible for making decisions on the project. I call this person the "Decider." In smaller startups, it's the CEO or a cofounder. In larger organizations, it might be the head of product, project lead, or senior vice president in charge of whatever. In short, it's the person in charge. Chances are, you know who this is.

If you're the Decider, great. If you're not, start by recruiting him or her. Sit down and explain why you believe the team will benefit from clearing the calendar to start the project right. Bring this book; it'll help.

In startups, getting the Decider involved is easy. As organizations grow, hierarchy gets complicated, and big decisions involve stressful high-stakes meetings. These internal pitches are a huge waste of effort and stress. If you instead get the Decider directly involved in sprints, you can focus everyone's energy on making your project click with customers—not on playing internal politics. Not only that, but the Decider contributes his or her insight when it's most valuable: right as the strategy is forming. It's a great use of their time *and* the team's.

Once the Decider supports the idea of a sprint, he or she can pave the way for assembling the rest of the team and clearing the schedule. Then, in the sprint, the Decider will speed the process along by making key decisions. Best of all, when the sprint is over, you don't have to convince the boss of the outcome, because the boss was in the room all along.

Form a tiny team

The Foundation Sprint compresses a whole lot of action into a short period of time. To move fast, keep the team small. I recommend no more than five people, including the Decider. Look for contrasting perspectives: Instead of a CEO and four engineers, get the CEO, the head of engineering, the head of sales, the head of product, and the head of marketing. Competing perspectives lead to better decisions, but with more than five people the returns diminish rapidly.

Declare a good emergency

I've dealt with many emergencies in my life. I've broken bones, broken teeth, ruptured my spleen, and caught swine flu. I've had power outages, jury duty, and maybe worst of all, slow Wi-Fi. I've had my flight canceled. I've had cars that won't start. I've had to clean up after sick pets, like, RIGHT NOW. And I've experienced emergencies at work. I've been on teams who dropped everything to deal with software bugs, failing banks, and earthquakes. In each situation, I discovered that, regardless of what my calendar said, I *did* have several free hours today. I didn't think twice about canceling meetings and ignoring my inbox. I sent one of those "eject lever" messages: "*Hey, I'm totally focused on (the bad thing), so I have to cancel and I'll be slow to reply until it's done.*" Nobody gave me a hard time. When bad stuff happens, we all get it.

So, guess what? You can declare a state of emergency to make space for your sprints. It's just a good emergency instead of a bad one.

Good emergencies are real, but grossly underutilized, and getting the best start on a big project absolutely qualifies as a good emergency. You can even use the same style of "eject lever" message:

Hey, our team is totally focused on (our most important project), so I have to cancel and I'll be slow to reply until it's done.

The Decider should broadcast an "eject lever" message to everyone the sprint team interacts with. Every person on the team should use an "eject lever" message to clear their schedules—and for their email and messaging out-of-office status.

Once you've set expectations for those outside the sprint, it's time to prepare those on the sprint team for a different way of working.

Work alone together

Once you gather your team, everyone's natural inclination will be to have an open-ended group brainstorm. Don't let it happen.

The group brainstorm is our species' natural response to collaboration. Gather a bunch of hunter-gatherers from the Ice Age and ask them to build a hut, and you'll get a group brainstorm. Gather a bunch of Royal Society scientists from seventeenth-century England and ask them to come up with a business plan, and pretty soon they'll be shouting ideas and ordering out for sticky notes and pizza.

Group brainstorms are in our DNA. They're fun—at least, for extroverts. But they don't work. They produce mediocre ideas. They exclude those who aren't comfortable in the group, those who don't excel at verbal sales pitches, and those who do their best thinking in silence.

So when it's time for you and your team to collaborate, do NOT brainstorm out loud. Do NOT have an open-ended discussion. Instead, work alone together. Give each person time to generate proposals in silence, time to review others' proposals in silence, and time to form opinions and vote in silence.

Silent, parallel work is counterintuitive but profoundly effective. In Stockholm, it helped Serge, Mikael, and me do our best work. JZ and I have seen the difference it makes in sprints with more than 300 teams. In your Foundation Sprint, when you work alone together with your team, you will get more, higher-quality solutions and faster, better-considered decisions.

You'll find more ideas for working alone together throughout the following chapters, and specific instructions in the checklist at the end. For now, as you prepare for your sprint, let the team know this won't be a typical meeting: in the Foundation Sprint, they'll have time to think, and they are guaranteed an opportunity to share their opinion without fighting for airtime.

Get started, not perfect

The goal of the Foundation Sprint is not to come up with a perfect plan. The goal is to come up with a rough draft: a Founding Hypothesis that you can test right away. This means you don't have to get your strategy right on the first try. If you make a wrong decision—or several—you'll find out soon enough, when you show prototypes to customers. Then you can adjust.

So don't stress. Make proposals, make decisions, and move on. You're more likely to arrive at a solution that clicks if you start fast and run lots of experiments, rather than spending forever refining your hunch in hopes of guessing your way to a perfect plan.

Before your sprint begins, introduce the team to the concept of "Get started, not perfect." During the sprint, remind them often. And hey, any time you feel stuck in life, remind yourself—and if you see me, remind me. It's good advice, and we could all use it.

Once you've formed a sprint team, cleared the calendar, and set expectations, you can immerse yourself in the sprint. I've seen teams do this hundreds of times, and people inside and outside the sprint embrace it, because focus is inspiring.

But free time alone does not guarantee results. In the next chapter, we'll start the Foundation Sprint—and I'll share an important lesson I learned from Tom Hanks.

Basics

Why are we doing this project?

Start the Foundation Sprint by establishing the Basics: who your customer is, the problem you want to help them solve, your team's unique advantages, and your strongest competition.

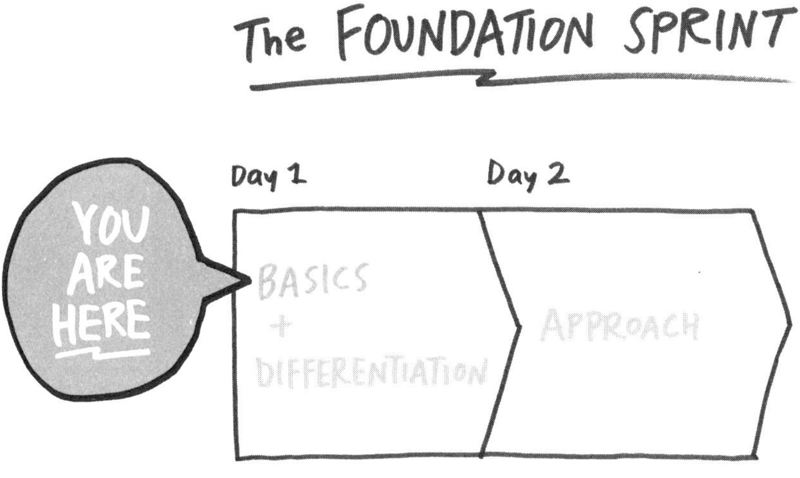
The FOUNDATION SPRINT
Day 1
Day 2
YOU ARE HERE
BASICS + DIFFERENTIATION
APPROACH

2

Customer

The first day of the Foundation Sprint begins with a sequence of questions called the Basics. I *love* the Basics, because the answers to these questions create a crisp picture of the project. They also take me back to a classic moment in a classic film.

In the 1988 movie *Big,* a twelve-year-old boy named Josh makes a wish and wakes up the next morning as a grown-up. The grown-up Josh, played by Tom Hanks, is forced to navigate the adult world and ends up landing a job at a toy company.

My favorite scene features Josh in a boring meeting. One executive makes a long-winded case for his pet project: a new line of toys that transform from robots into skyscrapers. He drones on and on about focus groups ("a double-blind format of eight overlapping demographics") and sales projections ("thirty-seven percent market share . . . one-quarter of total revenue . . ."). Meanwhile, Josh—the kid trapped in a man's body—plays with the skyscraper robot, his expression growing more and more confused.

At the end of the presentation, Josh raises his hand.

"I don't get it," he says.

Annoyed, the executive shoves a printout at Josh and rattles off more jargon. "If you had read your industry breakdown, you would see that our success in the action-figure area has climbed from twenty-seven percent to forty-five percent in the last two years."

But Josh presses his case. "There's a million robots that turn into something," he says. "What's fun about playing with a *building*?"

I was about twelve years old when I saw *Big*, and it formed my expectations about how the work world operated. I gotta tell you, it's not far off.

In the executive's presentation, he talks a lot about what the toy's sales could do for the *company*, but doesn't say a thing about what the toy could do for *kids*.

And in real life?

A lot of projects out there are Skyscraper Robots. We focus on what *we* want rather than what we can do for our customers. We put profits and ego first, losing sight of the fact that if customers don't care, there won't *be* any money or glory at all.

I know this is true, because I've done it. Before the sprint in Stockholm, I spent months designing a complicated 3-D conference room—not because it solved a problem for the customer, but because it was the product *I* thought would be cool. I mean, honestly, when have you ever been on a video call and thought, "Gosh, I could connect on a deeper level with my colleagues, if only this interface had a simulated wood-grain table"? What was I thinking? It's absurd!

But absurdity—and worse—happens when we don't put the customer first. This brings me to the second key lesson for making things click:

2. Start by identifying your customer and a real problem you can solve.

I use the word *customer* on purpose. Growing up, I spent years working in restaurants as a busboy, and as I set and cleared tables and filled coffee cups and water glasses by the thousands, the word *customer* came to have a special meaning for me. A customer was a guest, and I was their host. It was my job to serve; to make sure he or she had everything necessary for a great experience. It was my job to solve my customers' problems—ideally, before they occurred.

Not every team treats their customers as honored guests. But they should. JZ and I have seen the inner workings of many companies. The most successful teams respect, understand, and focus on their customers. Teams who see their customers as a pair of eyeballs and a wallet? They struggle. It's hard to make a product click if you don't care about the person it's supposed to click *with.*

Sure, there are exceptions, but not many. And ironically, even if they turn a profit, those who focus more on themselves than their customers are the least satisfied with their work. Squeezing people for attention and money is fool's gold. If you're playing the odds, bet on respect.

Since JZ and I are playing the odds—since we want the startups in our portfolio to be as successful as possible—we start the Foundation Sprint by identifying the target customer and the problem to be solved.

②

Start by identifying your customer & a real problem you can solve.

So, tell me: Who's your customer? What problem are you solving for them? These are obvious questions—almost rude. But again, the obvious stuff is not always so obvious. Most teams never clearly identify the Basics. They never test their ideas with their customers. They never get to know the people they're trying to help. Don't let it happen to you—not knowing your customer is the surest way to build a Skyscraper Robot that nobody wants.

The Basics are the first fiber in a thread that will lead to differentiation and a successful strategy. The Basics also give you the opportunity to start out idealistic, with your customers at the heart of your work. They ensure you're solving a problem you care about.

Here are some techniques for identifying your target customer and the problem you're trying to solve:

Use the Note-and-Vote instead of a group brainstorm

We created a method called the Note-and-Vote to help teams quickly find good ideas and make decisions. Mark this page, because you'll use the Note-and-Vote a bunch of times throughout the Foundation Sprint. It works like this:

1. **Question**—Ask the team a question. For example, "Who are our customers?"
2. **Silent work**—Give everyone about five minutes to think in silence and write as many answers as they can, each on a separate sticky note. Keep these proposals anonymous (don't put your name on the sticky notes).
3. **Silent share**—Put the sticky notes up where everyone can see. There may be duplicates; that's fine.

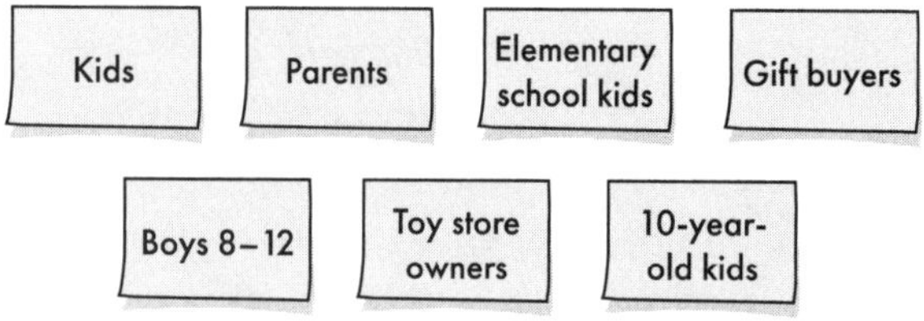

4. **Silent vote**—Each person reviews the sticky notes in silence for about five minutes and places two or three votes for their favorite proposals.

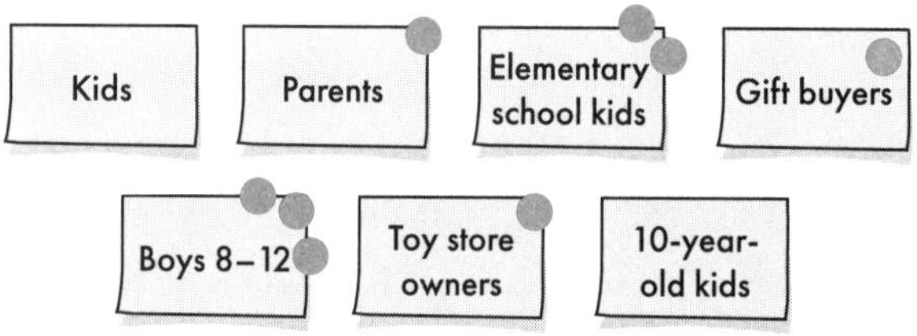

5. **Debate**—If the Decider isn't certain, they may call for a short debate about the top proposals.
6. **Decide**—The Decider chooses one proposal. They do not have to follow the votes.

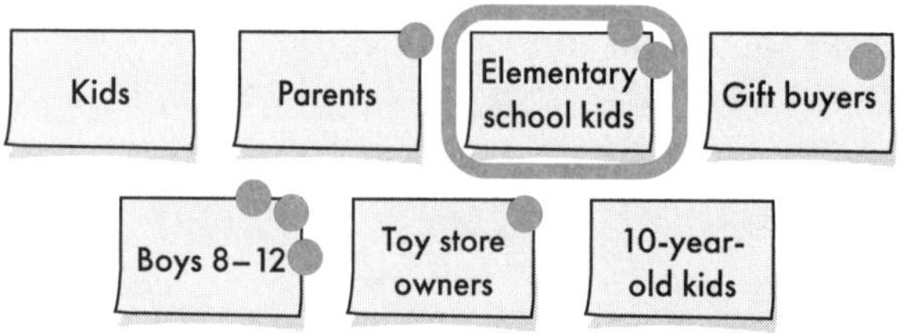

NOTE-AND-VOTE
?
1 ASK A QUESTION
2 SILENT WORK
3 SILENT SHARE
4 SILENT VOTE
?
5 DEBATE
6 DECIDE

That's the Note-and-Vote. You can Note-and-Vote to define your customer, then do it again to define the problem you're solving.

We use this collaboration recipe in different forms throughout the Foundation Sprint. The Note-and-Vote is a little awkward at first, but it quickly becomes second nature—and it's well worth the effort to learn, because this mode of working is much more effective than group brainstorming.

With a conventional group brainstorm, one idea jumps out—either because it's the first reasonable suggestion or because it's presented by the loudest voice—and then that idea dominates the discussion. Group brainstorms are a highway to ~~hell~~ consensus. Not just consensus, but *mediocre* consensus.

With a Note-and-Vote, you boost quality by tapping the power of working alone together. Each person develops opinions independently, without trying to talk and think at the same time (which I, for one, cannot do). And, because the proposals are anonymous, you can vote, debate, and decide without worrying about flattering or offending your colleagues.

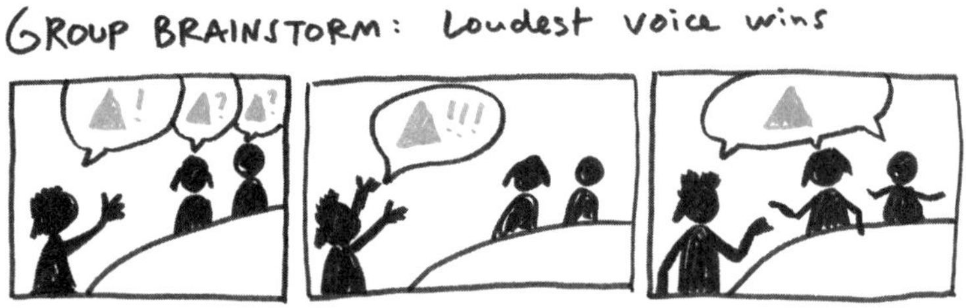

In addition to the quality of the proposals, the depth of the participation, and the honesty of the discussion, the Note-and-Vote has another important advantage: It's WAY faster than group brainstorms and open-ended discussions. I predict you'll love it.

We've led hundreds—maybe thousands!—of these Note-and-Votes, and we find that they work best if you use two simple tricks: plain language and the common sense test.

Use plain language

In *Big*, who are the toy company's customers? "Eight overlapping demographics"? That doesn't mean anything. Technical or business jargon creates a barrier of abstraction between the team and their customers. It obscures what's going on, and often, what it obscures is a strategy that's full of fluff.

Whenever possible, replace jargon with plain language. You'll be more precise, you can be sure that everyone on the team understands what you're talking about, and you're more likely to make decisions that make sense.

For Google Meet, our target customer could have been defined with some fancy-pants moniker like "distributed enterprise orgs," but "teams with people in different locations" works a lot better. Instead of "eight overlapping demographics," just say something like "kids in elementary school." Keep it simple.

Take the common sense test

When you're finished identifying the customer and problem, ask the team: "Does this make sense?"

Your answers shouldn't bend reality. For example, if I said Google Meet's customers were "3-D aficionados" and the problem was "lack of convincing wood grain on 3-D conference tables," anybody could see that doesn't make sense.

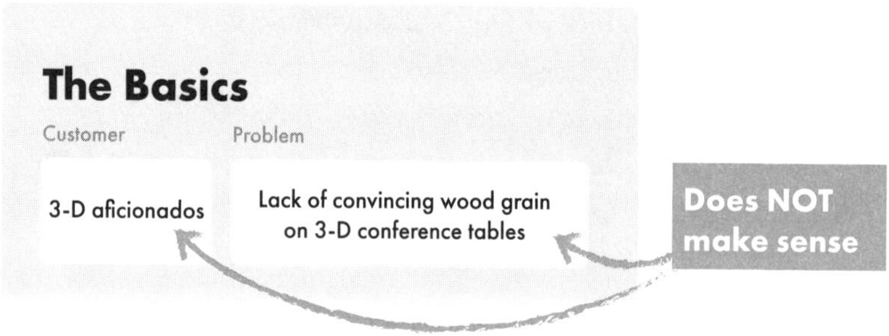

Customers should be real people. Problems should be real problems. In the case of Google Meet, our customers were teams with people in different locations and their problem was simply that it was difficult to meet. They didn't need wood grain, they just needed to easily connect with each other. Again: keep it simple.

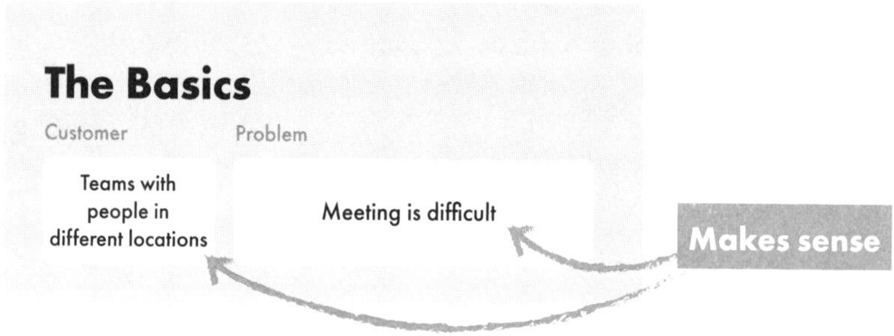

With your customer defined and at the center of your attention, your team is on the same page. You know who you want to help. You know what problem you want to solve. You have clarity. If you change your target later, after running experiments, that's fine—you're getting started, not perfect—but these simple decisions put you on the golden path toward a product that clicks, and toward work that is truly meaningful.

You can find more details about running these activities in the checklist at the end of the book. For now, it's time to move on, and in the next chapter, we'll go one step deeper into the Basics. I'll introduce you to a startup bringing artificial intelligence into messy real-world environments, and share a lesson that is even *more* obvious—and, as a result, even harder to see.

3

Advantage

We all have things we do well—and things we don't do so well. Topics we care about, and others that make us shrug. And we all have some set of ideas about the world that make perfect sense to us, but may be incomprehensible or just seem flat-out wrong to others.

Some of these differences are just differences. But some are advantages—and some of those advantages are *big* advantages, the kind that can help you create a solution to your customers' problem that nobody else can.

The next step of the Foundation Sprint is explicitly identifying your team's advantages—so you can figure out how to capitalize on those advantages to create a solution that clicks. To put it another way:

3. Take advantage of your advantages.

Surprisingly, most teams don't follow this obvious advice. Instead, they mimic existing solutions and play by other people's rules. When you ignore your advantages, you slip into the swamp of mediocrity. But when you take advantage of your advantages, you can rise up and stand out.

So what *are* your advantages? They come in three different flavors: **capability**, **motivation**, and **insight**. To show you how these different kinds of advantages work, let me take you back to the year 2014 and introduce you to three people who eventually became startup founders. As we go, see if you can identify the advantages they bring to their projects—and take a guess at what kind of company each might eventually create.

First, meet Katie Hoffman, a mechanical engineer.

On a typical day in 2014, we find Katie navigating among various kinds of industrial equipment, her hands covered in dust and grime, her eyes trained on a mass of cables that run from one piece of machinery to the next. Katie is in charge of a team who retrofits industrial plants with new control systems to optimize their performance. A big part of that job is figuring out how the old systems work, which, it turns out, *never* matches the design documents.

The cable she's following connects to yet another sensor not listed in the plant's documentation. Katie takes a photo with her phone, jots down a note, and sighs. Cracking the riddle of the old systems and improving their efficiency is satisfying—but in the back of her mind, she knows that someone else will be here in a few years, doing another retrofit, tearing out all of *her* work. In the meantime, the system will be static, never improving until that next major overhaul. To Katie, that reality seems like such a waste, and she's convinced there has to be a better way. But how?

③

Take advantage
of your advantages.

• • •

Next, meet Jim Gao—also a mechanical engineer.

On a typical day in 2014, we find Jim sitting in the control room of a huge Google data center in Iowa. Jim helped design this data center, but today, like Katie, he's searching for ways to improve its performance.

Pipes and conduits run in every direction, painted bright blue, green, red, and yellow. The data center looks like a *Super Mario* game come to life, only instead of toadstools and flying turtles, there's just row after row of server racks.

All day and all night, seven days a week and twelve months a year, cool water gushes through the multicolored pipes, absorbing heat from the servers and carrying it away. The pipes are doing their job, but as he reviews the readings in the control room, Jim can't help but feel disappointed. The system just uses *so much* electricity. Every time the server racks begin to heat up, the team who runs the data center revs up the cooling system output. That revving uses more and more energy, but there is simply no way around it—if the servers get hot, they shut down, and the internet goes dark. Maybe the inefficiency is unavoidable. Maybe he's come to the limit of what engineering can accomplish. All the same, something nags at Jim. What is he missing?

Finally, meet Veda Panneershelvam, a computer scientist.

On a typical day in 2014, Veda is sitting at a desk in London, writing code. Veda works with a team of world-class software engineers, and together they're digging into what was considered the holy grail of artificial-intelligence research: creating a computer program that can beat a human master at the board game Go.

If you're not familiar with Go, just know that it's complex. There are 10^{123} possible moves in chess, but there are 10^{360} possible moves in

Go. That's ridiculous. There are more possible configurations of a Go board than there are atoms in the universe!

To master Go, Veda and his colleagues must develop a new approach to artificial intelligence. They need to create a program that can see the future. In 2014, that seems impossible to most people, but to Veda, it's just exciting. The way he looks at it, if AI could master Go, there is no telling what other kinds of problems it might be able to solve for people.

Let's review, starting with customers and problems:

- Katie is solving inefficient industrial control systems for big manufacturers.
- Jim is solving electricity-guzzling data centers for Google.
- Veda is solving . . . hmm. I don't think he's really solving Go. I think the problem he's solving is actually the brain's limited capacity to deal with complex problems, and I think his "customer" is humanity. I know, that sounds a bit grandiose, but I think it's right.

Okay, what are Katie's, Jim's, and Veda's special advantages? Like I said, there are three kinds.

First up is **capability**. Capability is what you can do that few can match. If you work for a big company, you might have the capability of a well-known brand or plenty of money for your project; if you work for a tiny startup, you might have the capability to focus and move fast. But quite often the most relevant capabilities are just good old-fashioned know-how:

- Katie's an expert at mechanical engineering, with a focus on industrial controls.
- Jim's also an expert at mechanical engineering, with a focus on data centers.

- Veda's an expert at computer science, with a focus on artificial intelligence.

Katie, Jim, and Veda are all world-class at what they do—the Caitlin Clarks and LeBron Jameses of their fields—but their capabilities alone don't give us the full picture of their unique advantages.

Next, let's look at the second kind of advantage: **motivation**. Motivation is the specific reason you're going after this problem; a fire that burns bright in you but not in others. Motivation is relevant because it turbocharges capability, pointing the way to where and how you should use your strengths.

All three of these future founders were motivated to solve big problems and make a positive change. That's admirable, but it's also vague. I mean, sure, lots of people want to "make the world a better place"—but it's only when motivation gets specific that it helps you make decisions about what to do. So let's get more specific:

- Katie was frustrated by traditional retrofits of industrial controls.
- Jim was frustrated by the limitations of physical systems.
- Veda wanted to use AI to solve massive problems for humanity.

Notice that, for two of the three, the primary fuel was *frustration*. If that's your motivation, hey, that's okay. Some of the world's best products were created by people who were aggravated, vexed, galled, rankled, or driven bananas by the status quo. You don't have to start with a grand vision. Fury works.

Okay, with capability *and* motivation combined, these future founders' advantages become more unique. But what kind of company might each one create? Let's follow their stories a little further to find out.

• • •

Two years later, on March 9, 2016, Veda stood in a conference room at the Four Seasons Hotel in Seoul, South Korea, his eyes fixed on a live video stream of two men playing a game of Go.

On one side of the table was Lee Sedol, a professional Go player and eighteen-time world champion. On the other side was an amateur, who was a colleague of Veda's.

As Veda watched, his colleague set a white stone on the board. Veda's attention jumped back to the conference room. Here, computer monitors displayed dozens of graphs. The "win probability" chart ticked upward in favor of white.

The computer believed that Lee, the seemingly invincible champion, could be defeated.

Over the past few days, Veda and his teammates—fifteen computer scientists fresh off a flight from London—had converted this conference room into a makeshift control center. The purpose of the operation was to feed plays from AlphaGo, the artificial intelligence program they had created, to Veda's colleague, who would then execute those plays on the real-life Go board.

The winner of the match would win a $1 million prize. The whole setup might have been the premise for a caper movie—*Ocean's Fifteen*, anyone?—except it was no secret that Lee was playing against an AI. The referees knew it. Lee knew it. Everyone knew it. The match was being broadcast around the world, and millions were watching, even though most Go experts considered the game to be far too complex for a computer to master.

But on that March day in Seoul, AlphaGo won.

Thousands of miles away, Jim Gao was still searching for a better way to optimize the cooling systems in Google's data centers. He stumbled on the AlphaGo story as it was unfolding, got hooked, and began following the updates from Seoul with rapt attention.

As he dug into the details, he learned that the AlphaGo AI used a breakthrough approach called "deep reinforcement learning." A wild idea popped into Jim's head. Could deep reinforcement learning help with data center cooling? After all, finding the optimal configuration of controls at any given time was kind of like finding the optimal move in a game of Go.

It turned out that Veda and his teammates worked for DeepMind—a company owned by Google. Jim was thrilled—they hadn't met, but technically, they were all colleagues. So he emailed the DeepMind team and explained his wild idea.

Veda thought the data center challenge was fascinating, and he agreed to give it a shot. Over the course of several intense weeks, Veda, Jim, and a team of DeepMind engineers created a new deep reinforcement learning program. Then they put this new artificial intelligence in charge of the cooling system at a Google data center.

At first, the electricity usage spiked. The AI was experimenting, adjusting control settings at random like a toddler mashing buttons on a car stereo. But, like a toddler, the AI was learning. It reinforced the tactics that proved efficient. It improved. And improved. And improved some more, until, like AlphaGo, it was superhuman. Eventually the AI reduced electricity usage in Google's data centers by 40 percent.

I'll continue the story in a moment, but first, look at what happened when Veda joined forces with Jim. Their combined capabilities—Jim's data center expertise plus Veda's artificial intelligence wizardry—allowed them to build something that neither could create on his own. That's the power of unique advantages in action. But wait. It gets better.

• • •

In 2019, Jim and Veda met Katie—the mechanical engineer who was an expert at retrofitting industrial control systems—and the three of them started talking about how to reduce energy waste in the world outside Google. Factories and industrial plants use vast quantities of electricity on heating, cooling, and operating all kinds of equipment. Could AI help there, too?

For their part, Jim and Veda were convinced that they could radically improve energy usage in these plants—but they would need Katie's real-world expertise in order to design, sell, and implement a solution. Katie had led engineering and innovation teams at companies like Trane, Ingersoll-Rand, and Raytheon. She knew how manufacturers made decisions, and she knew the shortcomings of industrial controls. The world of industrial plants was a much messier landscape than the tightly designed Google data centers with which Jim and Veda were familiar—but it was a world Katie knew well. So they decided to go for it. The three of them left their jobs. At the end of 2019, they founded a startup called Phaidra.

Phaidra was one of our first investments at Character Capital, and their story is one of the big inspirations for the Foundation Sprint. They started with an audacious project: to make all kinds of industrial plants more efficient with AI. They tested ideas, learned how to build trust with customers, and made their first sale. They deployed a pilot program at a major pharmaceutical manufacturer; then, the following year, they won their first big contract and deployed their AI at five industrial plants. They eventually expanded their service to data centers. Today the superhuman, adaptive, future-predicting systems that Veda, Jim, and Katie all longed for back in 2014 are a reality.

To get there, they needed the third type of advantage: insight.

Insight is a deep understanding of the problem and of customers. Insight gives you a perspective that others just don't have. Jim had insight into data centers, and Veda had insight into deep reinforcement learning, but what unlocked Phaidra's strategy was Katie's insight into how industrial plants—and the companies who run them—operate.

When you combine the capabilities and insight of the three Phaidra founders, you get something special. You can think of it as an equation:

capability + insight + motivation = unique advantage

When Katie, Jim, and Veda met, they thought, "Holy smokes! Look at what we can do together!" Phaidra may be an extreme example, but you can create your own "Holy smokes!" moment with your own team and your own advantages.

Like the "customer + problem" questions from the last chapter, advantages can be so obvious that they're invisible. Once we assemble our team, we take for granted that we've got the right stuff. We don't crow about how good we are—who wants to hang around with a bunch of self-involved braggarts? We don't ask our teammates to remind us why they're qualified. That would be rude and weird.

But when those basic, obvious, foundational qualifications fade from view, you lose a terrific decision-making tool. Your team's advantage shapes your strategy by pointing the way to a special solution that your team—and *only* your team—can deliver.

Identify your team's unique advantage

The next element of the Basics is your team's advantage.

Once again, you'll work alone together. Once again, you'll follow the Note-and-Vote steps—only this time, give answers in three categories: capability, insight, and motivation. What special skills set your team apart? What unique understanding do you have? And what's your motivation—of all the things you could do with your one human life, why this?

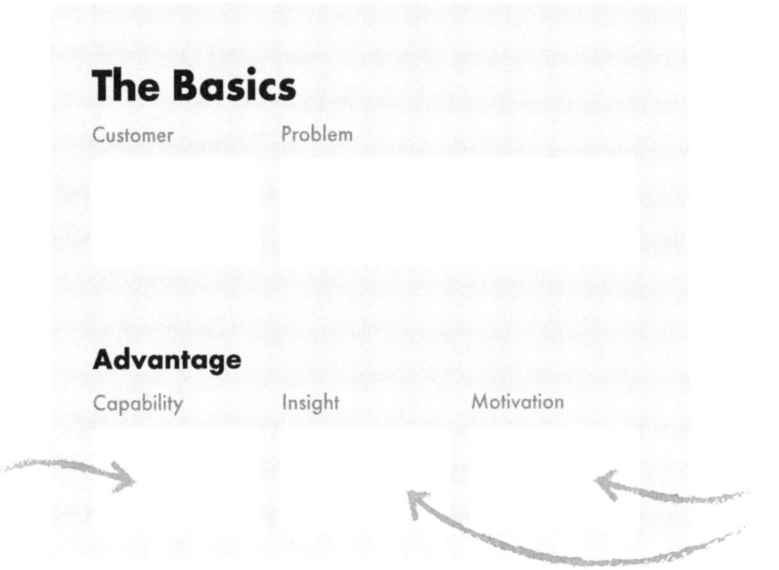

When creating Google Meet, our team's capability was web and video engineering. Our special insight was that, as a remote team ourselves, we understood the need for easy meetings. Our motivation was making it so people could work together, no matter where they lived.

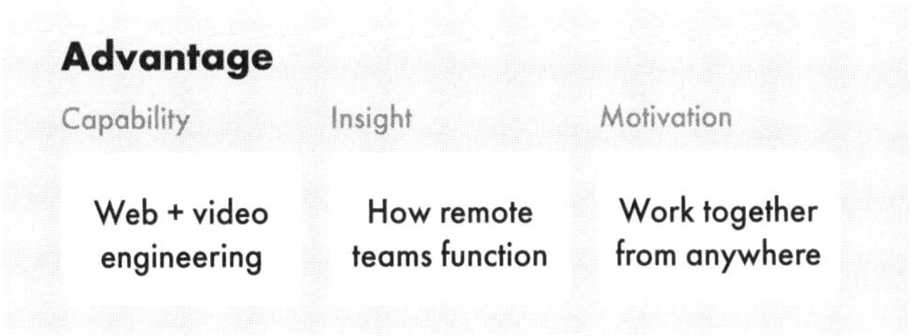
Advantage
Capability
Insight
Motivation
Web + video engineering
How remote teams function
Work together from anywhere

Phaidra's unique capability was a combination of computer science and mechanical engineering. They had special insight into how industrial plants operated. Their motivation was saving energy.

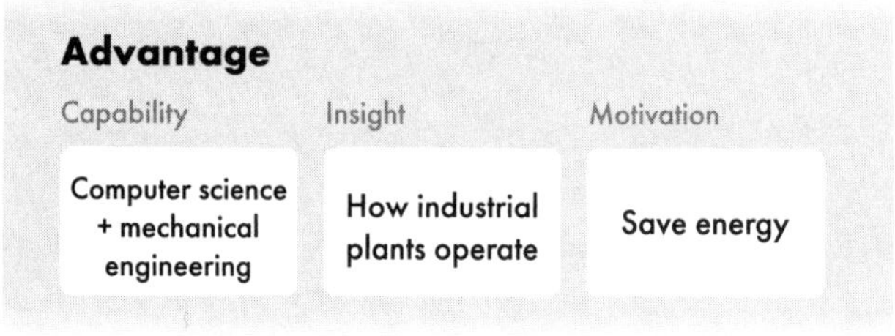

Just as you did for the customer and problem, you'll write down answers and vote in silence, then have the Decider decide. He or she should choose one most important advantage in each category. Look for capabilities, insights, and motivations that make your team unique—and tough to beat. Later, you'll think about how to use those advantages to set your solution apart from the competition.

In the next chapter, I'll ask you to shift your gaze. To understand your advantages, we've looked inward, but to craft a successful strategy, you must look outside your team and make an honest assessment of the competition and alternatives. To illustrate this idea, I'll tell a story about the most powerful mom in the history of sports.

4

Competition

When I was a kid, the world's biggest star was Michael Jordan and the world's coolest company was Nike, because they made his signature Air Jordan shoes. I'd work all summer just to buy the latest pair. Did it matter that I was a die-hard Seattle SuperSonics fan, but Jordan played for the Chicago Bulls? No, it did not. Jordan wasn't just a basketball player, he was a deity, and his shoes were divine.

Even though I'm now (supposedly) a grown-up, I still collect Air Jordans. I still think they're beautiful. I still get a thrill when I slide them on my feet. I'm a sneakerhead—one of those enthusiasts/weirdos who has a closet full of shoes, tracks every 1980s rerelease on Nike's SNKRS app, and would wear Air Jordans to a wedding, if I were ever invited to weddings.

So when JZ told me there was a movie about how Nike signed Jordan in the first place? I had to see it.

The film, called *Air*, takes place in 1984, before Jordan became world-famous. Back then he was just an outstanding college player about to start his pro career. As for Nike? It was the third-place basketball shoe company, behind Converse and Adidas.

In 1984, the best pro players—Magic Johnson, Larry Bird, and Julius "Dr. J" Irving—wore Converse. Adidas was the cool brand, the shoes that a young Michael Jordan wanted to wear in his free time. Nike had a paltry 15 percent of the market for basketball shoes.

The story opens with a talent scout named Sonny Vacarro (played by Matt Damon) evaluating college basketball players whom Nike might be able to sign. Back then, Nike had only a small budget for sponsoring basketball players, so Sonny is bargain-hunting—until he sees video footage of Jordan. In the movie, Sonny is all alone, late at night, watching and rewatching a clip of Jordan hitting a game-winning shot. Sonny is enthralled. He notices something special in that clip, and his intuition tells him that Michael Jordan will be not just a successful player, but a generational talent, an unprecedented superstar. He realizes before almost everyone else that Michael Jordan is, well, *Michael Jordan*.

But Nike can't afford to sign Jordan. And even if they had the money, Nike's too uncool. Jordan is dead set on signing with Adidas. Converse is his backup plan. He won't even agree to *meet* with Nike.

What follows is, essentially, a sprint. Sonny has only days to change Jordan's mind. Sonny needs a winning strategy, fast.

Like the teams we work with, he starts with the customer problem: Sonny's customer is Michael Jordan. Jordan's problem? On the surface, it's "How do I get the best shoe deal?" But Sonny recognizes that Jordan is special, so his problem is more like, "How do I get the most out of being a superstar?"

Sonny has special insight—he sees something in Jordan that others do not. And Nike is desperate. They're in last place. They're motivated by frustration. So, inspired and outgunned, Sonny breaks all the rules. He convinces Nike founder Phil Knight (Ben Affleck) to abandon the plan of signing several athletes and instead offer the entire basketball budget to Jordan. He convinces Nike designer Peter Moore to do something unheard of—design a signature basketball shoe for a rookie. Not only that, but, against the wishes of Jordan's agent, Sonny goes so far as to visit Jordan's parents at their home in North Carolina—uninvited.

In North Carolina, he realizes something big: his real customer is not Michael Jordan, it's Jordan's mom, Deloris (Viola Davis). She is the one he has to convince. Sitting across the table from Deloris, with the Jordans slated to meet Converse and Adidas in a matter of days, Sonny decides this moment is his only chance to change her mind.

"I'll make a bet with you," he says. "I'll tell you exactly how those meetings are gonna go. And if I'm wrong, then don't take a meeting with Nike. But if I'm right, please consider that you and Michael come out." He goes on to predict that Converse won't have a plan for making Jordan stand out from Magic, Bird, and Dr. J. He predicts that Adidas' leadership will appear disorganized—a problem, he points out, that will cause headaches for Jordan in the future.

I don't think I'll spoil the movie for you if I give away the ending, because everyone knows what happened. Sonny's predictions come true, and Michael and Deloris agree to visit Nike. Deloris tells Nike they'll have to give Michael Jordan a cut of the revenue, they agree, and it's a deal. Sonny pulls off the impossible.

One of my favorite scenes is the fateful meeting in Oregon when the Nike team unveils the signature shoe.

The first Air Jordan was black, red, and white. (The color scheme violated NBA rules, but Nike paid Jordan's fines.) The shoe is a work of art, with a bold design and elegant lines. When Michael Jordan held it in his hands for the first time? It clicked. Watching it happen on-screen, this sneakerhead got goose bumps.

But it's that backyard conversation between Sonny and Deloris that is the key moment in the movie. Sonny's knowledge of the competition earns Deloris's respect. And in that conversation, Sonny foreshadows how his knowledge of the competition will shape Nike's winning strategy. Adidas looks disorganized? Nike will demonstrate its vision with an over-the-top offer. Converse won't put Jordan above its other stars? Nike will do the unprecedented and give Jordan his own shoe.

Nike's strategy illustrates another important lesson for making things click:

4. Get real about the competition.

The next step in the Foundation Sprint is identifying the competition. Like the other Basics, this is so obvious that most teams skip it when forming their strategy. Or they dismiss the competition, naively assuming their new solution will be so good that customers will forget the alternatives.

So how should *you* figure out the competition for your project? To help you make sense of who you're up against, and why your solution is superior, you can once again use the Note-and-Vote method. Work together in silence, generate options, and vote before the Decider chooses the most important competitors. Give your team the following guidance:

④

Get real about the competition.

Start with direct competitors

First, write down the other companies or products that more or less solve your customer's problem. This is the standard definition of "competitor," and it should be easy. Nike knew they were up against Converse and Adidas because those companies were the market leaders.

Start with the competitors you already know about. If you can't think of many, do some research. But don't dig too deep. Well-known alternatives are the ones you're competing with in customers' minds.

If you can't find any competitors, that could be a warning sign. Management consultants might call it a "green field opportunity," but management consultants don't live in the real world. No competition usually means there's not a real problem.

Search for substitutes

Sometimes there's no direct competition because customers are solving the problem using a *substitute* solution. Phaidra's AI for industrial plants didn't compete with other AIs for industrial plants. Instead, manufacturers used a work-around: their engineers manually adjusted systems to optimize performance. That's what Phaidra had to beat.

If there is no direct competition, but customers *are* using substitutes, it could be a big opportunity. Breakthrough products are more likely to compete with substitutes than direct competitors. When Netflix's streaming service launched, they weren't going head-to-head with equivalent products, but there were plenty of other ways to watch movies (remember DVDs and TiVo?)

Write down a list of substitute products, alternatives, and work-arounds that customers use to solve their problem. These can be harder to identify than direct competitors, but you can always just go ask your customers. The question "Hey, how do you solve this problem today?" is remarkably effective—and if you don't hear an answer that includes time or money or both, it's probably not a problem worth solving.

Or you might be competing against nothing

Remember how I JUST said that no competition usually means there's not a real problem? Well, the word *usually* is key. Usually, no competition means the team is deluding itself. But sometimes customers do have a real problem; it's just that nobody has offered a reasonable solution yet. In these situations, you're competing with *nothing*. These are the riskiest opportunities, but also the most exciting.

At Character Capital, we encountered this situation with a startup that made it easy for small businesses to calculate their carbon footprint. When we did this step in a Foundation Sprint with the team, they realized that the "competition" they were up against was . . . their customers doing nothing and feeling bad about it. So they wrote that down and took their best shot at designing a product that was *better* than doing nothing.

In the end, the startup abandoned the carbon-accounting idea because not enough small businesses were willing to pay for their product. As I said, it's risky competing with nothing! In this case, the startup learned that "do nothing and feel bad about it" was tough to beat, and pivoted in another direction.

Another Character investment, a startup called House Rx, helps medical clinics set up in-house pharmacies so that patients with complex or chronic conditions can more easily get the specialty medications they need. Before House Rx developed their solution, it was impossible for clinics to run their own pharmacy—so they, too, were competing against "do nothing." But in this case, their strategy clicked. They designed a service that offered so much value to clinics and their patients that they overcame the inertia of "do nothing." It can be done, and it can lead to something awesome, but don't expect it to be easy.

Go for the gorilla

Whether you have lots of competitors or just a few, you should pay special attention to the strongest, toughest, biggest alternative—the eight-hundred-pound gorilla that wants to solve your customers' problem.

In early 2015, we ran sprints with Slack to help them prepare for their first big marketing campaign. At the time, Slack was still a new product, and most potential customers had never heard of it. The app had a few direct competitors: other niche business apps who offered instant messaging. But none of those newcomers were well known.*

So, instead of positioning themselves against small-time competition, Slack picked the biggest fight they could find. They compared themselves to the undisputed heavyweight champion of business communication: email. Their marketing strategy focused on convincing customers that life was better without email, and their product strategy focused on making it easy for teams to quit email and switch to Slack. Picking a big fight worked—just nine months later, Slack's user base had quadrupled from 500,000 to over 2 million.

Setting your sights high will push you to create the best possible solution. Sonny didn't tell Deloris Jordan how Nike was better than Keds or New Balance, because those companies weren't serious contenders. To make your solution click, you'll have to stand out from the best.

At this point, we're halfway through day one of the Foundation Sprint. We've covered all the Basics: customer, problem, advantage, and competition.

Now it's time to use your knowledge of the Basics to figure out your differentiation—that is, what sets you apart from the competition. In the next chapter, I'll show you just how to do that, and I'll introduce you to another startup with a business plan that sounds like science fiction, so we can see how they use differentiation to get the attention of skeptical customers.

*This was long before Microsoft launched Teams, a product with remarkably similar functionality to Slack, including, entirely coincidentally, the same purple color scheme.

The Basics

Customer

Problem

Advantage

Capability

Insight

Motivation

Competition

800-pound gorilla

Top alternatives

Differentiation

why should
customers care?

Design **differentiation** that will set you far apart from the competition, then write project **principles** to bring your differentiation to life.

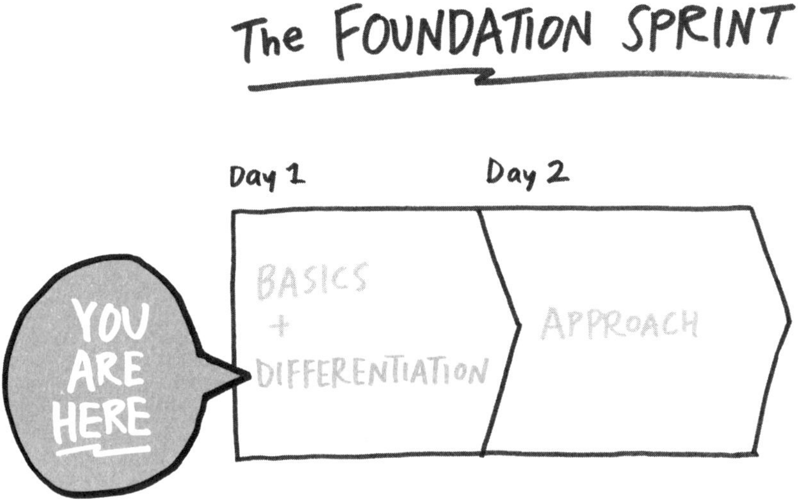
The FOUNDATION SPRINT
Day 1
Day 2
BASICS
+
DIFFERENTIATION
APPROACH
YOU
ARE
HERE

5

Differentiation

When I first met Jonny Godwin, founder of Orbital Materials, he told me that his company was going to invent new molecules. I was like, record scratch, *Invent new molecules?* What does that even mean, and how could it be a business?

Jonny had a good explanation. First, he listed examples of man-made materials from the twentieth century: Metal alloys enabled space travel. Jet fuel propelled commercial flight. Nylon made parachutes that helped turn the tide in World War II.

The twenty-first century, he said, has plenty of challenges that could be solved by the next wave of new materials. But there's a problem. The art of material development is still stuck in the last century. It's slow and unreliable, depending on loads of trial and error with a side order of luck. It can take years and go nowhere.

To speed up the process, Jonny and his team would use artificial intelligence. They believed that miracle materials—like a cobalt replacement for lithium batteries, or a cheaper and more abundant alternative to jet fuel—could be invented and synthesized in a fraction of the time with the help of AI.

Like Veda from Phaidra (Chapter 3), Jonny worked at Google's DeepMind, where he led the creation of an AI that analyzed X-ray scans to diagnose breast cancer (the program was so effective that it outperformed radiologists). He left Google and teamed up with an all-star team of AI experts, chemists, and molecular scientists to form Orbital Materials. Within a few months, they made a stunning technology breakthrough in the lab, where they synthesized something called a "template molecule." Synthesizing a template molecule usually takes over a year. It took Jonny and his team just five weeks.

The Orbital Materials team was confident their technology could work, but for their fledgling company to survive they had to build trust with customers: large chemical companies who would help bring Orbital's new molecules out of the labs and into the world. Character Capital is an investor in Orbital Materials, and at this moment—when they were trying to develop an offering that clicked with customers—we ran a Foundation Sprint together.

For Orbital Materials, the "competition" was the traditional, trial-and-error way of developing new molecules. The traditional way had two big advantages: it was familiar, and manufacturers were already doing it. From his earliest conversations with potential customers, Jonny knew that, seen through this lens, his solution—which required a whole new way of working—didn't have a chance. The promise of Orbital's technology just wasn't getting through.

Let's look at how Orbital compared to the competition with a simple 2x2 chart:

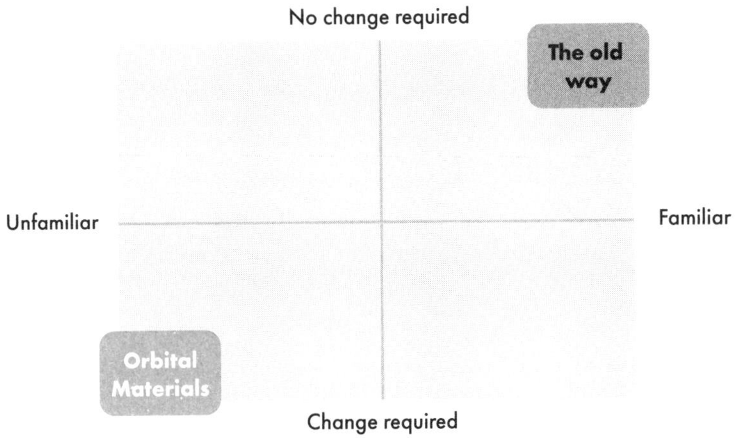

How could Orbital create an opening with manufacturers? They had already tried a kitchen-sink approach to sales, firing off to customers a dozen unique benefits of their technology, but the barrage of ideas was overwhelming.

Jonny decided to focus on two factors they identified during their Foundation Sprint: quality and reliability. These factors weren't as splashy as speed. But "higher quality" and "lower failure rates" were immediate, practical benefits. The message was simple, and with Orbital's unique advantage—outstanding capabilities in both computer science and chemistry—they could back up the sales pitch with credible details.

Right after their Foundation Sprint, the team made a new slide deck, then tested the pitch with customers. Instead of having ten or twenty different ways to talk about Orbital Materials, they spent their effort proving just two assertions, making detailed arguments for why both were true.

Let's look at this new way of framing Orbital Materials against the competition:

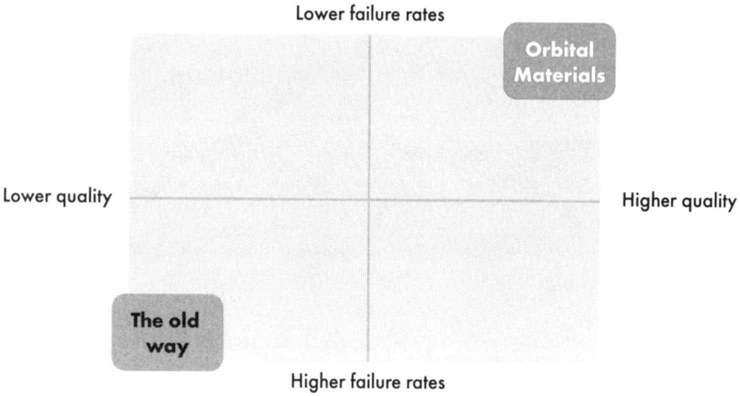

This new framework? It was clear. It was simple. It made sense to manufacturers. After a few more conversations, Orbital Materials signed up their first pilot customers. And the framework became more than just a sales pitch—from that point on, the Orbital Materials team emphasized reliability and quality as they built their technology, so they could be sure to deliver what customers wanted.

The Orbital Materials story illustrates the next essential lesson:

5. Differentiation makes products click.

When you create a new product or service, you're asking people to make a change, and every change has a cost. To get people to pay that cost—whether it's money, time, effort, risk, stress, or just brainpower—your solution must stand out.

That's where differentiation comes in. Differentiation is . . . well, it's what makes your product or service *different* from the alternatives. It's the essence of your solution; the most important message that

⑤

Differentiation makes products click.

customers need to understand. It's how you capture customers' attention, and why they switch. It's what makes your solution click.

The most successful products don't just differentiate a little—they create radical separation from the competition. These products make a bold and exciting promise: "Try the new way, and it will blow the old way out of the water."

To do this, they offer customers not just a new solution, but a brand-new framework for evaluating solutions. They illuminate factors that people may never have considered, or may not have realized could be improved. The most successful products *change how customers see the world.*

Differentiation is for your customers, but it's also for you. It's the essence of your strategy; the most important thing your team needs to deliver. It's a North Star, a plan of action, and a decision-making guide, all rolled into one.

Next, let's reexamine the project that became Google Meet—because today, looking back after years of working with startups, it strikes me as a great example of differentiation in action.

In 2009, the major videoconferencing options were Skype, which was ubiquitous, and Tandberg, a high-end service with fancy hardware. Skype and Tandberg made for tough competition. Our fledgling project couldn't compete with Tandberg's video quality. And Google didn't have a giant network of existing video customers, like Skype.

If we make a 2x2 differentiation chart to show Google Meet's predicament in 2009, it looks pretty hopeless:

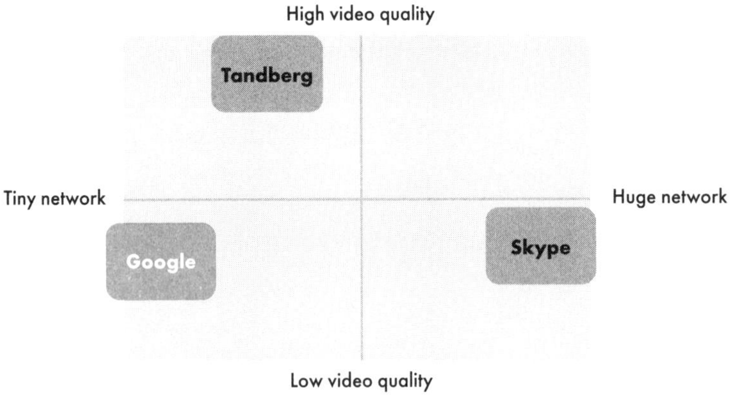

How could we reframe our work to have a chance at competing against two industry titans? During that week in Stockholm, we decided to ignore network size and video quality. Instead, we focused on ease of use. We designed a prototype that allowed multiple people to join a meeting just by following a web link. This strategy built on our advantages, including Google's capability at building web-based software and our team's motivation to make video meetings available to anyone—not just those who could afford a fancy setup. "Just a browser" and "multi-way" became the product's differentiation—and when customers saw it in action, it clicked.

Now, if we make a new diagram, the promise to customers is clear:

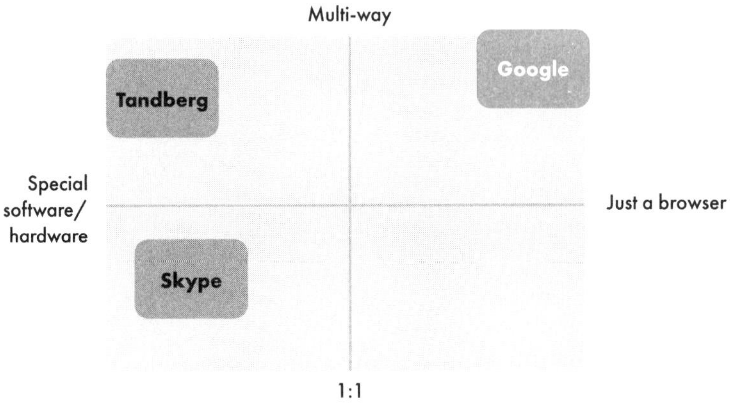

Strong differentiators can create a durable opening in the market. Even years later, Google Meet's differentiation holds up against Zoom, Microsoft Teams, and Apple's FaceTime. Sure, there are other criteria that are more important to some customers, but for those who value browser-based simplicity, Google Meet still stands out.

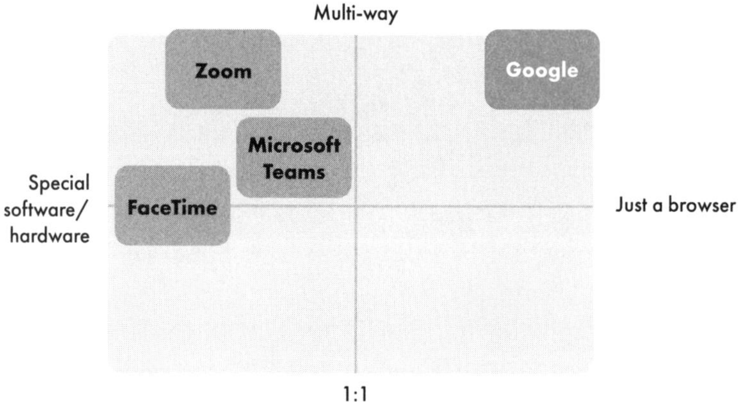

Video-call competition today

Once you start seeing the world through differentiation goggles, it's hard to stop. So let's make a few more diagrams. When Nike played the standard differentiation game against Converse and Adidas, they were in a horrible position. Their budget was too small, their brand too uncool. We can chart it like this:

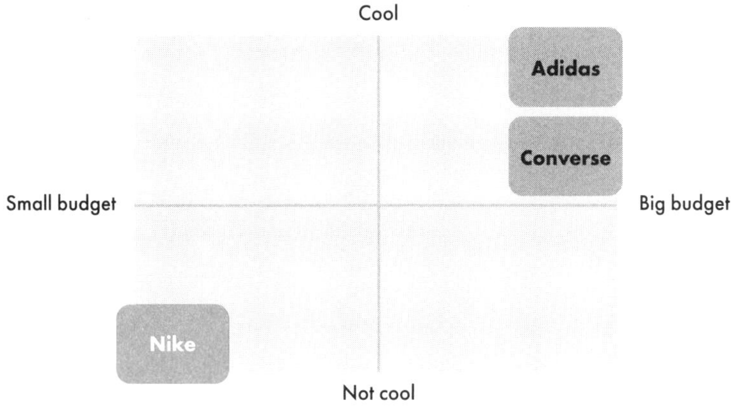

They differentiated from Converse and Adidas with a signature shoe and an unprecedented deal that included a cut of revenue. They changed the framework, and their offer clicked.

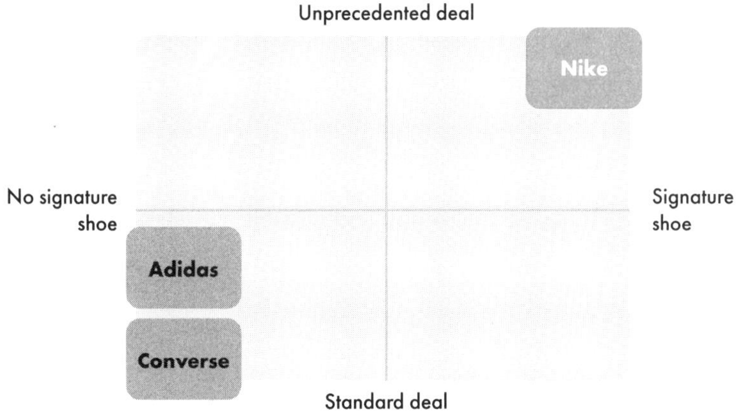

Slack was up against email, a familiar and reliable solution that customers had been using for years. Looking back, we can chart it like this:

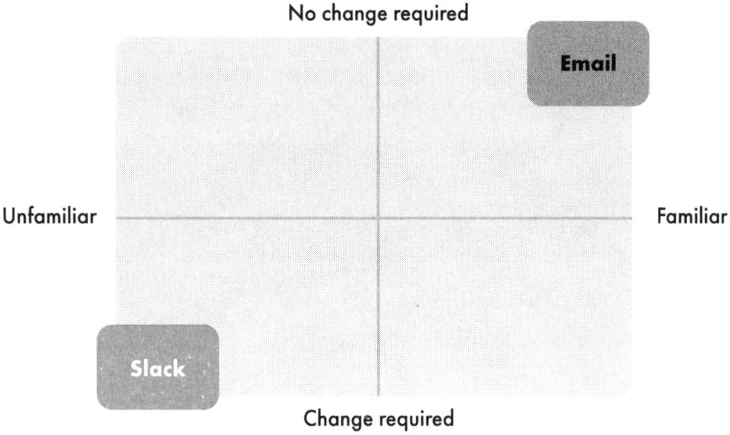

To differentiate, Slack focused on boosting teamwork and making communication fun. They reminded us why we all hate email, and showed us how different the world could be. The new framework clicked.

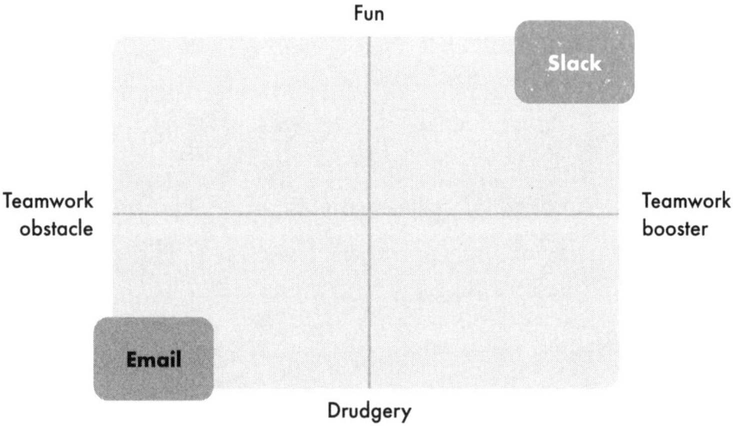

A startup called ASI—another Character investment—wanted to build software to help students study more effectively. Their competitors included quiz apps, traditional textbooks, and the eight-hundred-pound gorilla of studying: good old-fashioned paper and pencil.

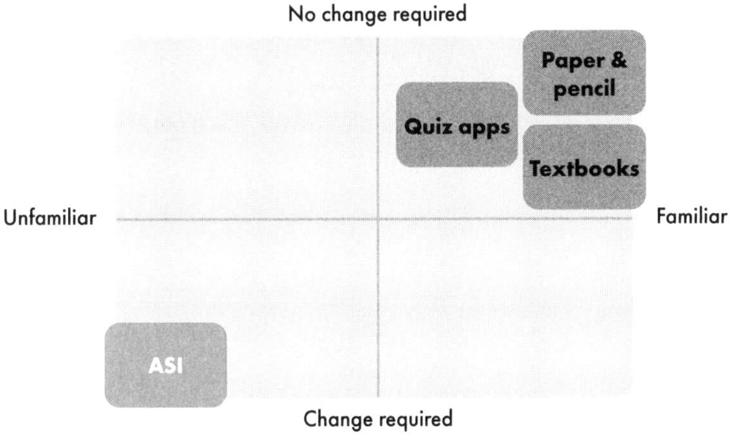

High school students aren't as set in their ways as chemical companies, but ASI still needed to create a new framework to show why their solution was better. So they decided to differentiate by giving students individually tailored study tools (rather than one-size-fits-all tools generated by a company) and by automating the process, so that it was faster and more effective than working with paper and pencil.

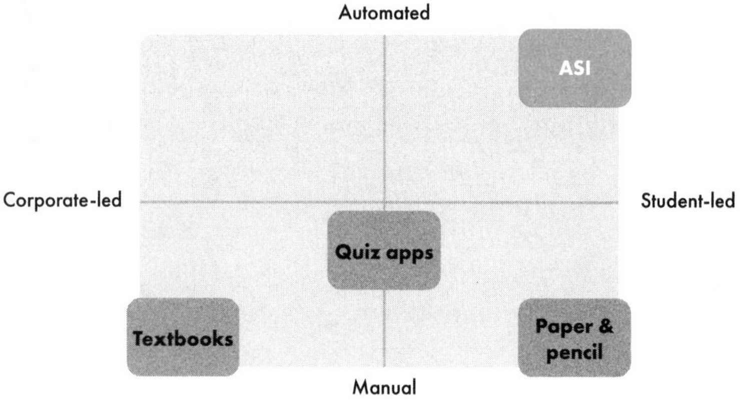

Differentiation looks different for every solution—that's kind of the point. But getting it right is always a big deal. No, strike that. It's a HUGE deal. Because, again, it helps both your customer and your team.

Differentiation helps your customers at every stage of their experience. At first, it helps them understand why your solution is worth learning about. Later, it helps them understand why it's worth adopting. Eventually, it helps them explain your solution to other people. Differentiation is a throughline from the moment you start building your product to the moment customers encounter your new creation to the moment they recommend it to someone else.

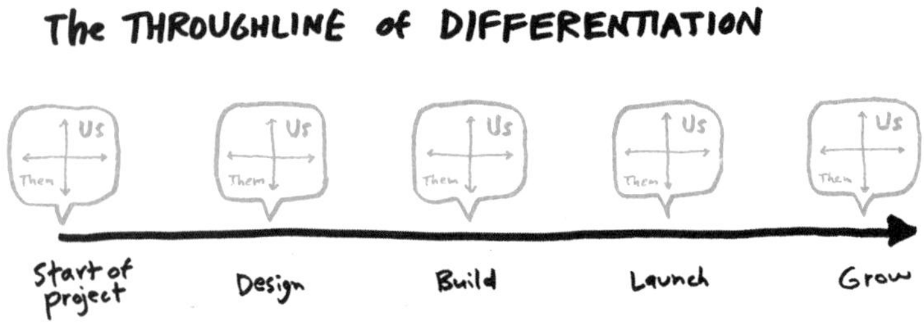

Differentiation also energizes your team. To explain what I mean, consider the opposite: a project that copies the competition and offers nothing special to customers. Working on that irrelevant project would probably feel uninspiring and demoralizing. What's the point of giving your best effort if nobody cares about the result?

But with clear differentiation, the team comes alive. They know what they're building and why it's exciting. They know why they work *here* and not for the competition. Doing something that's never been done before, something that will matter to customers? That's invigorating. As our cofounder Eli says, "Differentiation builds clarity and momentum."

So how should you figure out your project's differentiation? Here's how we do it in a Foundation Sprint:

Use your unique advantage

The best differentiators are at the intersection of what is super valuable to customers and what you can uniquely deliver. Even though it's obvious, I find it helpful to draw that as a Venn diagram for teams:

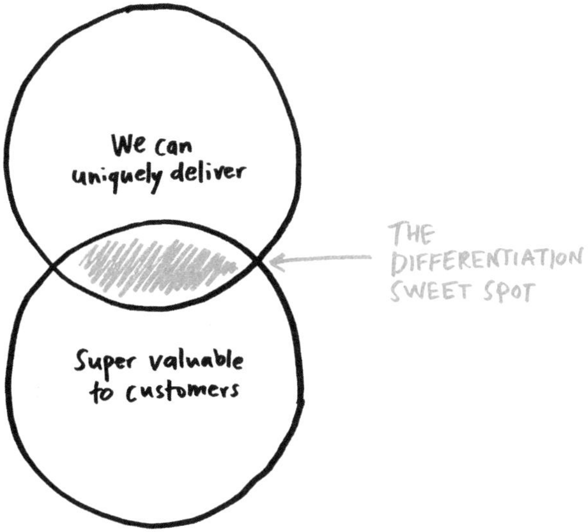

Start with "realistic optimism"

At the risk of sounding hippy-dippy, you gotta start in the right mindset. If you're too negative, you'll sell your team short and miss the best differentiators. If you're overly optimistic, you'll pick dream-world differentiators that are unachievable. Instead, use *realistic optimism.* This is no compromise—it's pure optimism; it's just tethered to reality.

Here's how to do it: Imagine the project is finished and everything went as well as possible. You're still the same team, in the same real world, but on this project you did everything right. You came up with a great strategy, maximized your team's advantages, and overcame all difficulties along the way. You pitched the perfect game—or, for Harry Potter fans, you drank a bottle of the Felix Felicis potion. Now, shift your gaze to your customers and imagine that, in this perfect version of the real world, you created the most valuable possible change for them. What might that world look like for your customers? That's realistic optimism.

Follow our differentiation recipe

I have to level with you: Finding great differentiators ain't easy. It requires deep thought, considering multiple perspectives, and experimentation. That's why most leaders and teams don't ever get to great differentiation—which is too bad, because they miss out on all the benefits I outlined earlier.

It's not easy, but it's also not rocket science. The way I see it, great differentiation is like making pizza from scratch. If you have the right recipe and ingredients, and you're willing to give a special effort, anybody can do it.

Try to win on the classics

Great pizza needs great toppings, and you should always consider the classics: mozzarella, tomatoes, basil, olive oil.

Similarly, you should always consider the classic differentiators: fast vs. slow, easy vs. difficult, free vs. expensive, focused vs. unfocused, simple vs. complicated, integrated vs. siloed, automatic vs. manual, and smart vs. not so smart. If you can win on any of these, that's great, because these differentiators are tried and true. People generally understand them right away and respond well to them. (Especially "free." We're all crazy about "free.")

Go through all the classics and consider how your solution might stack up against the competition. Where could your product be on the spectrum from fast to slow? Easy to difficult? Free to expensive? Remember, this doesn't have to describe where you are now, but where you could be when the best version of your project is complete. Be realistically optimistic. Working alone together, each person places a dot on each spectrum.

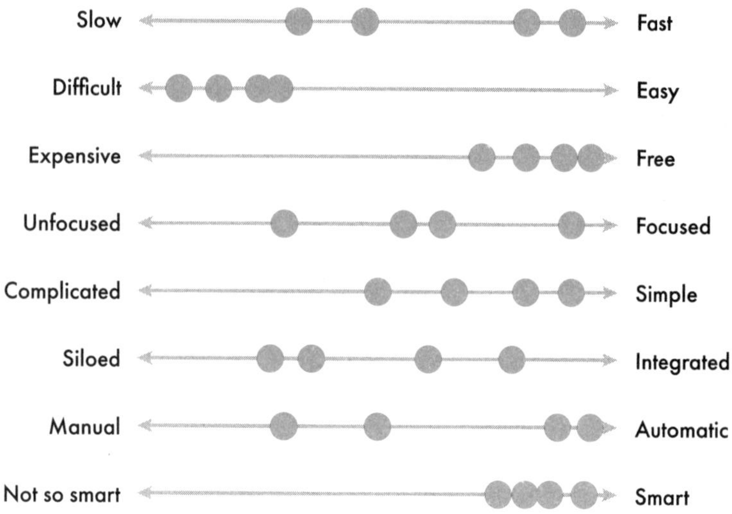

Choose your own differentiators

Next, go beyond the classics and come up with your own customized differentiators. Think pineapple, feta cheese, anchovies—not for everyone, maybe, but for the right person? Irresistible.

So what do you believe matters most to your customers? What factor could make your solution unique—and, importantly, what crummy opposite attribute could describe the competition? Once again, work alone together so that each person has a chance to create their own scales.

After the team creates custom "good vs. crummy" pairings, work alone together to place dots on the new scales. It's okay if you end up with some dots on the "wrong" end of a spectrum—the purpose of this step is to find the differentiators where you really stand out from the competition, but not every one will work.

Finally, the Decider chooses her or his top two differentiators. Here's how this looked for Orbital Materials, the startup using AI to design molecules:

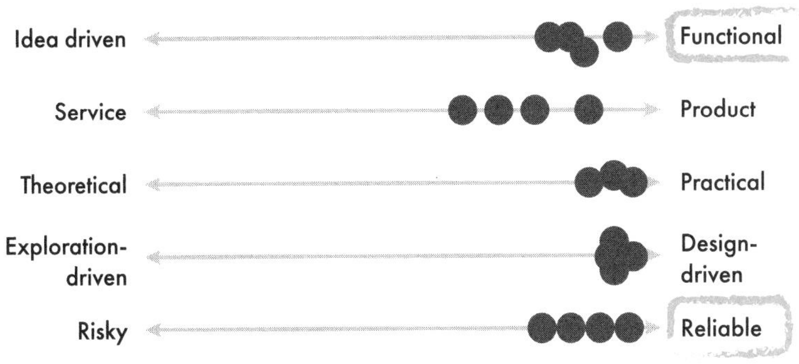

Make a 2x2 chart with extreme differentiation

In 2007, Steve Jobs walked onstage to introduce a new product. He put up a slide with what he called a "business school 101 graph." One axis went from *smart* to *not so smart*; the other from *easy to use* to *hard to use*. Jobs proceeded to fill out the graph with the competition. Regular cell phones (remember those?) weren't smart, he said, but they also weren't that easy to use. Smartphones (in 2007) were kind of smart, but even harder to use than regular cell phones. "We don't want to do either one of those things," he said. "We want to make a leapfrog product that is *way* smarter than any mobile device has ever been, and super easy to use." He pointed at the top right corner, where a single word appeared: "iPhone."

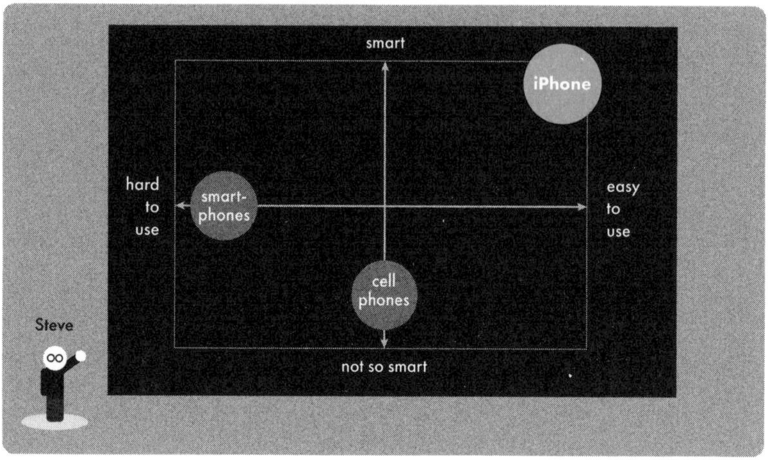

That slide wasn't just marketing fluff. You can bet there was as much emphasis on *easy to use* during the development of the iPhone as there was onstage. That's something at which Apple still excels: they build the same thing that they market. There is one throughline from development to delivery, and it's focused on the customer.

I want you and your team to have Jobs-like clarity, and a 2x2 chart of your own is a powerful tool to help you get there. So, once you've chosen your top two differentiators—whether they're classic or custom—make a 2x2 chart, place your project in the top right, place the top competitors on there, and adjust your differentiators until it's realistic, optimistic, and you've got the top right quadrant to yourself.

Now, if you're a skeptic, I get it. We've all seen mediocre 2x2s. They're usually throwaway slide-deck fillers, hastily created and short-lived. They typically focus on technology, logistics, industry . . . everything but the most important thing: Customer perception. And in these mediocre 2x2s, the magic upper right quadrant is often littered with alternatives.

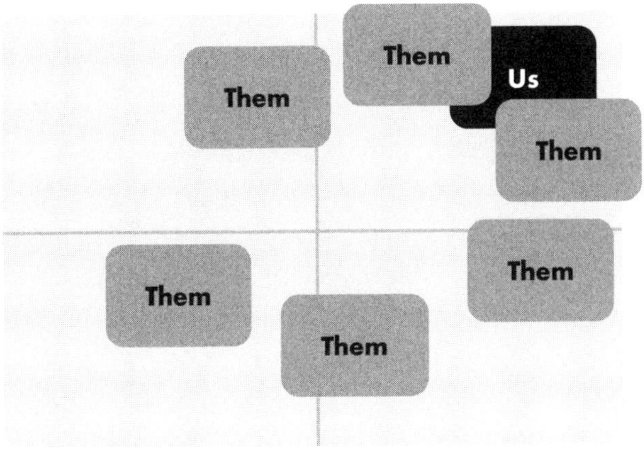

This is not good enough. If you're only 3 percent better than the competition, it won't be worth the calories for your customers to even *think* about trying your product. Make it an easy decision for them. When you create your 2x2, keep trying until you find differentiators that put you all alone in that top right quadrant and push the competition into the other three quadrants (which form an L shape that I like to think of as Loserville).

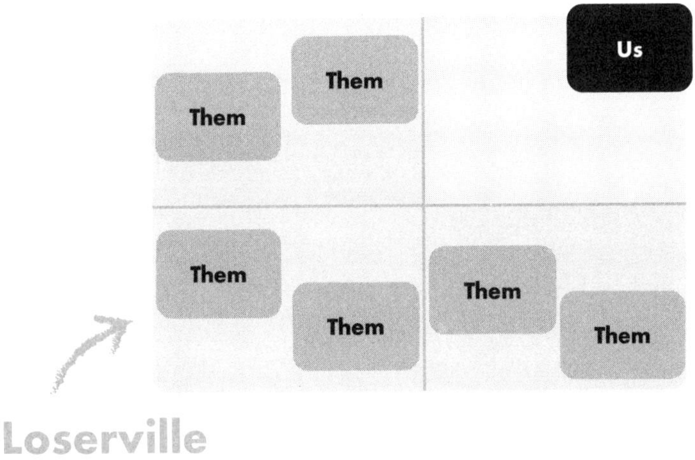

But be honest. No hype or baloney. Differentiation only works if you deliver on your promise. Most leaders and teams don't get the differentiators right on the first try, so don't worry if it takes some effort. Differentiating ain't easy.

If you're honest about the strengths of the competition and your own advantages, and if you put in the time to find the right factors, the 2x2 differentiation chart is a simple, clear, and powerful method of stating your strategy. Of course, it's still just a hypothesis and you still have to prove it, but it's a fantastic way to start.

A great 2x2 chart can become a beacon for everyone who interacts with the project. The leaders will know exactly what value they're creating for their customers, the builders will know what they're building, the marketers will know what they're selling, the buyers will know what they're buying, and the recommenders will know what they're recommending. You'll make a million decisions during your project, and this simple chart can help you make the right choices by reminding you of what matters most.

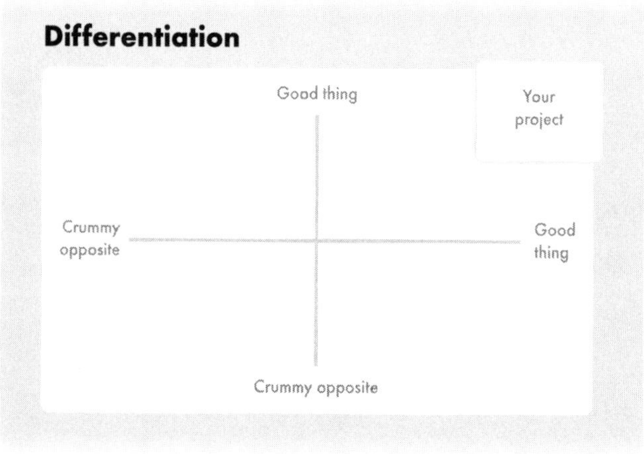

We've come to the end of the chapter, but we're not done with differentiation. In the next chapter, we'll wrap up day one of the Foundation Sprint, and I'll share another decision-making tool that is often used but rarely used well—and show you how it can bring your differentiation to life.

6

Principles

On a sunny Monday in January 2007, I was one of a few dozen new employees at Google's headquarters in Mountain View, California. The orientation staff handed out garish propeller hats in blue, yellow, red, and green with the word *Noogler* (short for "new Googler") stitched on the front.* They showed us presentations about how the search engine worked. They also introduced us to a document called "Ten Things We've Found to Be True."

"Ten Things" was a list of lessons learned in Google's first years. To be honest, not all of them were memorable, and some (like #9, "You can be serious without a suit") were kind of confusing. But the first three were solid gold. Here they are:

*If you stumble on any photographic evidence of me wearing that hat, do me a favor and destroy it?

1. Focus on the user and all else will follow
2. It's best to do one thing really, really well
3. Fast is better than slow

Later, when I worked on Gmail and Google Meet and led sprints for projects like Chrome, Photos, and Search, I'd hear people quoting these three statements. Engineers would quote them when talking at a whiteboard. Executives would quote them in product reviews. I learned to quote them, too.

These principles weren't just platitudes: they were a manifesto for decision-making. "Focus on the user" encouraged us to build the best possible experience for customers above all else. Instead of starting with a plan to squeeze money out of people and working backward toward delivering value, we should start with value and figure out the business later. "Do one thing" reminded us that Google was all about search, and everything we made should either revolve around search or, at the very least, have hyperfocused functionality of its own. "Fast is better than slow" was the easiest to understand and apply. We measured new features by milliseconds added or reduced. People loved Google because it was fast, not fancy, so we should consider how every decision would impact the speed of the customer experience.

Those principles and the decisions they influenced all reinforced Google's differentiation. Fast. Customer-focused. This is what separated Google from competitors like Yahoo!, MSN, and AOL. This is how its search engine became the front door of the internet.

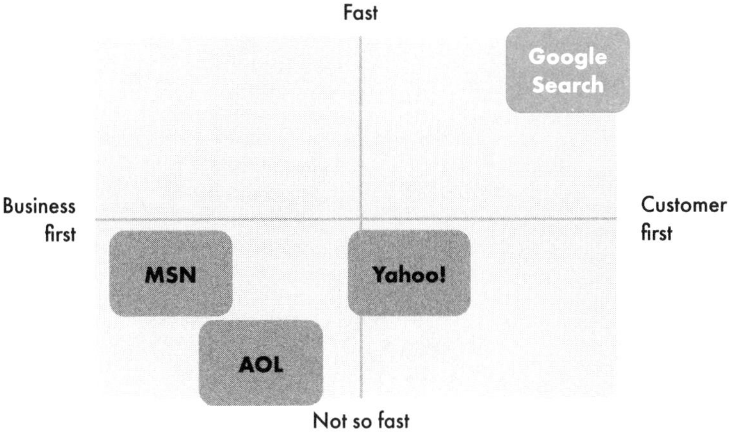

I've worked on teams that didn't have decision-making principles. We still made decisions, of course, but we had to create and re-create our decision-making criteria from scratch. Often, when ego and sales pitches took over, we made decisions without any criteria whatsoever. I'm not saying that never happened at Google—it'll happen anywhere—but "Focus on the user," "Do one thing," and "Fast is better" sped up decisions by offering authoritative criteria that everyone understood. And with every decision those principles influenced, they furthered Google's differentiation as the fastest and most useful way to get things done.

This experience taught me the next lesson for products that click:

6. Use practical principles to reinforce differentiation.

The word *practical* is important here. Like 2x2 charts, principles are common but rarely relevant. Plenty of teams have phrases like "pursue excellence" or "always be innovating" listed in some forgotten document, the dust-covered relic of a team off-site or a boss with too much spare time. They're well-intentioned but ignored.

⑥

Use practical principles to reinforce differentiation.

The trouble is not that these principles are too lofty—there's nothing wrong with being high-minded. No, the problem is that they're abstract. What does "Always be innovating" even mean? How does "You can be serious without a suit" help with forming strategy? Decision-making requires relevant opinions, not cultural clichés or vague ideals. "Focus on the user" is decision-making advice. "Do one thing" is decision-making advice. "Fast is better"? That's right, it's decision-making advice.

So how do you get practical decision-making principles for your own project? Here are our techniques:

Practical principles, not company principles

First, don't try to write company principles. Instead, keep it simple and just write principles to help with the project at hand.

One huge reason why the "big three" Google principles are useful is that they came from the earliest days of the company. They're a time capsule from an era when Google was a tiny startup who had to get every project right. As a result, the principles are imbued with a sense of urgency. That makes them easier to translate into action.

Or consider Apple's principles, written by Mike Markkula in 1977, when the company was a startup on the verge of launching its first major product, the Apple II. Paraphrasing, the three principles are:

1. Understand customer needs better than any other company
2. Eliminate unimportant opportunities
3. People DO judge a book by its cover

These aren't the principles of an established company with the luxury to sit around and describe how to treat one another nicely. This list is a survival guide. Sure, this manifesto just so happened to serve Apple well for decades, but it wasn't designed to do that. These principles were written for 1977, to get the Apple II out the door, into the world, and onto customers' desks. They were written to keep a tiny company from going bankrupt. Urgency is what made them great.

At the beginning of your project, there is no need to write timeless behavioral guidelines that will last a thousand years and fill future generations of employees with pride, courage, and warm fuzzies.

Right now, you're starting at zero, and what you need is a set of principles to guide you toward *one* product that clicks. And if you do that well? Hey, who knows, those survival principles might just last a lifetime.

Turn your differentiators into principles

When you create a 2x2 chart, you end up with two strong differentiators—which can easily turn into two strong principles. Here are a couple of examples from the Character portfolio companies you met in the last chapter:

- **ASI** turned their differentiator of "student-led" into the principle "Remove the fog in academic exploration." It's easy to imagine using this principle to make decisions: Does this particular feature give students more clarity as they explore a subject?
- **Orbital Materials** turned their differentiator of "functional" into the principle "A new material isn't a breakthrough without a chemical process." This principle reminded them to make each project decision with an eye toward the big picture: creating a repeatable process for chemical companies.

A handy trick for writing this kind of principle is to answer the question "What advice would I give a new team member to make sure we follow through on our differentiation?" That's what a good principle is: advice for your future self and your future team.

Differentiate, differentiate, safeguard

How many principles should you write? I think a good number is three. I suggest using the "Differentiate, differentiate, safeguard" formula: one principle for each of your two differentiators (from chapter 5), plus one to protect against the unintended consequences of building a product that's successful in an unfortunate way.

The only thing worse than a project that flops is one that clicks—but accidentally screws up customers' lives. Zooming out to the big picture of humanity, it's easy to see that we're continually transforming our daily lives with new technologies, services, and products. It's also easy to see that many of those transformations take more away from us than they give.

So, once you create a couple of principles to help make your product click, change your state of mind. Listen to some death metal and think about how you might make the world worse. Then see if you can't write a principle to make sure it doesn't happen.

Phaidra, the startup building AI for industrial plants, wrote the safeguard principle "Empower don't replace." They wanted to create a solution that would augment the skills of the engineers who run industrial plants, not put them out of work.

Perhaps the most famous example of a safeguard principle is Google's former motto, "Don't be evil." Over the years, outsiders poked a lot of fun at "Don't be evil." The company eventually dropped it in 2018. But back when I worked at Google, I thought it was pretty useful. It really jibed with the "Focus on the user" principle—it provided authoritative support to any argument that, above all else, we should never screw over our customers. "Don't be evil" wasn't perfect, but it was that rare cultural principle that helped with practical decisions. If you're tempted to write a cultural principle of your own, go for it. Just be sure to make it bold and useful.

Note-and-Vote to write your project principles

You don't need to talk to generate principles. If you work alone together, you can have it done in about half an hour. Just follow the usual process: give everyone a few minutes to think and compose as many potential principles as they can. Then vote, discuss, if needed, and let the Decider decide. In other words, it's just another Note-and-Vote.

Keep wordsmithing to a minimum

Wordsmithing, as I define it, means "revising and re-revising in search of the perfect phrasing." Listen, words matter. Getting the right phrasing is important, and I personally spend a lot of time doing it.

But we've all been in meetings where a group of people tried to wordsmith collaboratively, in real time, and it went on *way* too long. Sure, the first five minutes can have some real value as you identify phrases that are clear to one person but confusing to others. After that, additional wordsmithing becomes a surefire recipe for burning time and diluting your principles. ("Evil is so harsh. What if it said *Don't be mean*?")

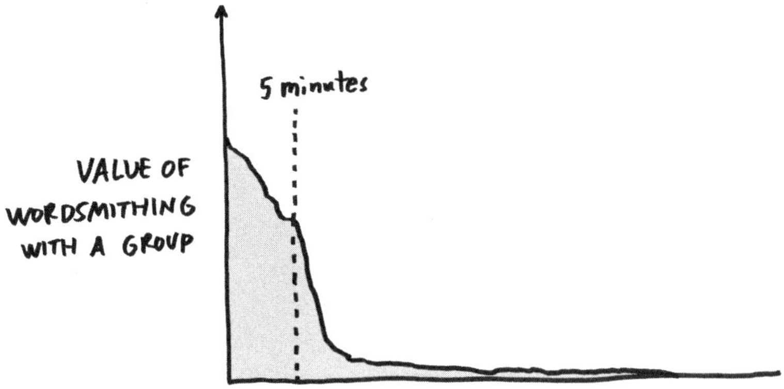

The best writing and editing is done by individuals thinking quietly, so don't spend more than five minutes on wordsmithing as a group. Remember that, at this stage, these project principles are experimental. You're not going to carve them in marble. So choose three, fix 'em quick, and get going.

Make a Mini Manifesto

Put your project principles and the 2x2 differentiation chart together, and you've got what I call the Mini Manifesto. It's an easy-to-understand guide for making decisions in the rest of the Foundation Sprint and beyond. Print it out and stick it on the wall.

Mini Manifesto

Differentiation

Principles

1

2

3

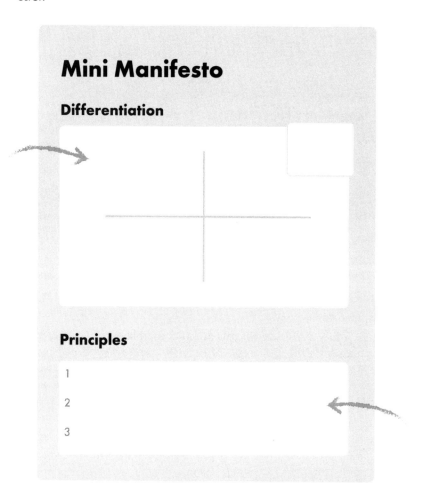

The Mini Manifesto marks the end of day one of the Foundation Sprint. For more detail on the schedule, see the checklist at the end of the book.

Day two of the Foundation Sprint is all about choosing the best approach for your project out of many possible paths. In the next chapter, I'll take you to the Swiss countryside for inspiration.

Approach

What's the best opportunity?

On day two of the Foundation Sprint, choose an approach to your project. Create multiple options, evaluate them through different lenses, and select one path to pursue first.

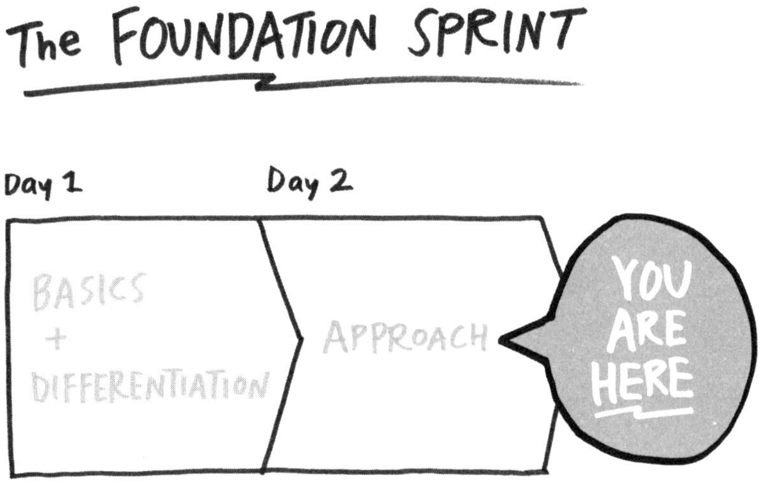
The FOUNDATION SPRINT
Day 1
Day 2
BASICS + DIFFERENTIATION
APPROACH
YOU ARE HERE

7

Options

The other day, I was writing—totally in the zone, keyboard clacking away—when I noticed that I was ravenously hungry. I wanted a cookie, and there's a bakery called Brown Bear just a few steps from my office. I hustled to their front door, but I'd lost track of time, and Brown Bear was already closed for the day. That's okay. I'm flexible. I crossed the street to Darvill's Bookstore, which has a great coffee bar that serves cookies. But Darvill's, too, was closed. That was a tough blow. I found enough inner strength to turn around and walk to the grocery store, where I bought an apple—which, in my opinion, is nature's cookie. Mission accomplished.

First strategies often fail, and when they do, we adjust and go in a different direction. Startups call this a "pivot."

Pivoting as you learn is smart. Very few products click with customers before pivoting at least once. Slack started out as a computer game called Glitch. Nike started out as Blue Ribbon Sports, an importer of Japanese running shoes.

Yes, pivoting is smart. However, it's also time-consuming. When I failed to get a cookie, it took only a few minutes to acquire an apple. But when a big project flops, it typically takes months—or longer—to try a different approach. Glitch took two years to build, and when it faltered, it was another two years before the launch of Slack. Blue Ribbon Sports scraped along for *seven years* as an importer before manufacturing the first Nike shoe.

Most teams don't have that kind of stamina. They run out of conviction, cohesion, motivation, and money long before they relaunch. But what if you could pivot before you even began?

On day two of the Foundation Sprint, you'll execute what you might think of as a "pre-pivot." Before you start heading down that first path, you'll stop, take a breath, and look to see if there are any other directions to consider. By the end of the day, you'll have an approach for your project—and a backup plan.

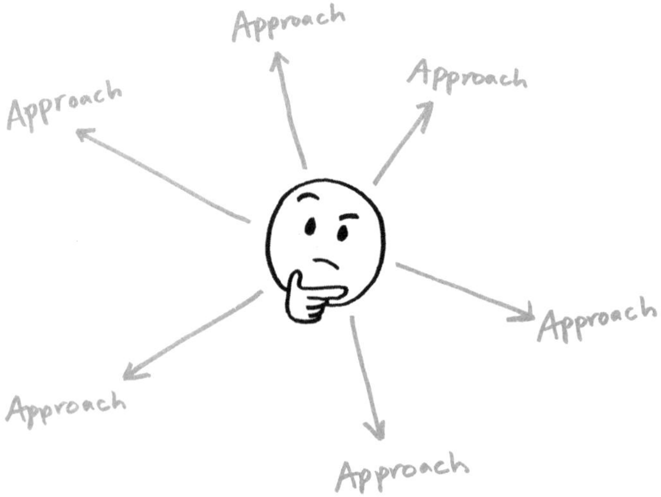

To show you how a pre-pivot looks, I'd like to tell you a story about a side project that grew into a sustainable business. As the tale unfolds, try to predict which approach the founders will pursue.

On an October afternoon in 2014, a young couple hiked in the countryside near Fribourg, Switzerland.

Those who have never visited Switzerland might imagine a stereotypical landscape—you know, Alps, cobblestones, chalets, rolling green hills dotted with cows, that kind of thing. In reality? Yeah. Switzerland looks *exactly* like that. The whole place is a postcard. And on this particular October afternoon, even the weather was postcard perfect. Not a cloud in the sky.

The couple, Eglé Minkstimaité and Stéph Cruchon, walked for hours. They discussed plans for their wedding. They talked about quitting their jobs and starting their own business. They strolled down cobblestone lanes, past charming chalets, and along rolling green hills.

Then they stumbled on something mysterious. It was the ruin of an old church, its stonework decaying beneath a tangle of vines and vegetation.

"What is this place?" Eglé said. She checked her phone, but the map showed nothing but a field of empty green pixels.

They approached the building, pulled back the greenery, and peered into the dim and dusty interior like explorers in an *Indiana Jones* movie. But there was no sign, no plaque, no inscription. Nothing.

"This place has to have a thousand stories," Stéph said. But there was no one around to ask. Reluctantly, they turned back.

Now, returning the way they came, they began to see mysteries everywhere they looked. They wanted to know the history behind this huge oak tree, that giant rock split in two, this forgotten medieval tower, that romantic bench. All these places seemed special. They, too, must have stories.

As they walked, Eglé and Stéph came up with an idea. Wouldn't it be cool, they said, if locals could record the stories behind small but intriguing landmarks? If visitors could easily access those stories, it would transform the experience of visiting a new place. It was easy to imagine that kind of product on a phone. But it was *so* obvious, they thought. Surely, if it doesn't already exist, someone will make it soon.

So they put it aside. They got married. They quit their jobs and started a consulting business. They had a kid. Years passed. That idea about a collection of local stories and secrets? Eglé and Stéph kept talking about it. It still seemed obvious to them, and they looked forward to the moment when someone would create it. But nobody ever did. Finally, in 2022—eight years after that walk—Eglé and Stéph decided it was up to them.

They founded a new company, called Genius Loci. They knew the project basics: Their customers were tourists and the problem was "finding hidden gems." The competition was Google Maps, Apple Maps, printed guidebooks, and local tour guides. Guidebooks and map apps didn't cover tiny places of interest, and while a local tour guide might, they were expensive and difficult to find for off-the-beaten-path sights. Genius Loci would differentiate by being deeply local and easily accessible. So far so good.

The clear-cut approach was to build an app that used GPS to find nearby points of interest. For years, whenever they thought about the hidden-gems problem, an app with GPS was the solution they envisioned, and Stéph was ready to start building it. But Eglé suggested they pause and consider new options before they committed to the app. After some debate, Stéph agreed.

So they came up with several alternate approaches. Instead of building an app with GPS, they could:

- Use a different technology instead of GPS
- Build a website instead of an app
- Make a physical solution (for example, signs installed at points of interest)
- Or some combination of the above

Physical signs sounded boring. A website would be far less magical than an app. As for a Frankenstein combination of the two? Yuck. But examining these alternate approaches revealed a critical flaw in Eglé and Stéph's original plan for Genius Loci.

An app with GPS would be incredibly easy to use, but *only if everything worked perfectly.* Every landmark would need correct GPS coordinates—not likely if local volunteers were filling in the data. Every landmark would need a strong cell phone signal so tourists could download the app—not likely for landmarks in the middle of nowhere. So an app would require a successful advertising campaign to ensure tourists had it on their phones *before* they encountered a hidden gem. An app with GPS could be magical, but that magic was fragile.

When they reviewed the entire menu of options, Eglé and Stéph recognized that the app alternatives, while unglamorous, were far more robust. For new users, it would be faster to load a website than install and set up a new app (especially with a shaky cell signal). Physical signs didn't require advertising. Either would be easy to build. Heck, they could create signs *and* a website in far less time than they could create an app.

In fact . . . maybe putting the two together was the way to go. When they first thought of creating a combination, they were scraping the bottom of the idea barrel, and the approach struck them as clunky. But now they reconsidered. The physical sign would point tourists to the website. In a way, it was elegant.

So they designed a simple, attractive physical sign: a stainless-steel badge with a QR code. Locals could affix these badges to points of interest. Tourists could scan the QR code with their phone to bring up a website featuring stories, video interviews with locals, and photos from the past.

They started selling the service to all kinds of organizations: tourism offices, village and city governments, parks, universities, even museums. Today you can find Genius Loci badges throughout Switzerland and France. The physical-digital combination clicked.

The story of Genius Loci illustrates our next simple lesson:

7. Seek alternatives to your first idea.

Questioning the project approach in the beginning can feel weird—like starting a road trip by exiting the highway to triple-check the map at a rest stop. "When Eglé suggested we consider other options, at first I thought she was crazy," Stéph says. "We knew the app was the best way to go. I was ready to build it."

Stéph's reaction makes sense. When we're excited about an idea, we want to accelerate, and applying the brakes goes against our instincts. But looking back, Stéph says he's glad they slowed down. "Yeah, turns out she was right," he says. "If we followed our first idea, it would have killed the company."

JZ and I recommend coming up with three or more options before deciding which approach to take. Here are some techniques for making your list:

Start with known options

If your team already has a bunch of ideas, you've got a head start on this exercise—just list out all the approaches that you've identified. For example:

- App with GPS
- Website

Imagine your approach fails—then what?

After you've written down your known options, come up with some new ones. If you feel stuck, try answering these questions: What would happen if your project hit a dead end? How would you solve your customers' problem if you couldn't do it the way you want?

Or imagine a new competitor comes along to solve the same problem for the same customer. How might they approach it?

⑦

Seek alternatives to your first idea.

For Genius Loci, the additional approaches would look like this:

- Physical signs
- App + signs
- Website + signs

Consider alternate customers

For some teams, the biggest question is not about the form of their product, it's about customers.

For example, the team from Phaidra, the startup building AI for industrial plants, believed they could boost efficiency in all kinds of facilities, but they needed to choose one to focus on first. They created a list of three customer options:

- Data centers
- Paper and pulp plants
- Chemical reactor plants

A Character portfolio company called Hypernatural was building tools to help people make fun videos with AI. Like Phaidra, they figured their solution would work for a variety of customers, but didn't know whom to focus on first. Here's their list of customer options:

- Small business owners
- Podcasters
- Video creators
- Marketing agencies

Boring is fine

It's totally okay if the options on your list seem obvious or even a bit boring. You're not trying to win a creativity contest here. You need viable approaches to your project, not razzle dazzle.

Write one-page summaries

Next, make a one-page summary for each approach. (If you have more than five, use a Note-and-Vote to narrow the list.)

The big idea with these one-page summaries is clarity. Never assume that everyone on the team understands what everyone else is talking about. The words "physical sign" might make one person think of a stainless-steel badge, but they might make another think of a tacky plastic billboard.

To make sure everyone is on the same page, fill out a page (ha!) explaining each approach. Be sure to include these three elements:

- The **title** of the approach.
- A one-sentence **summary** of why it's a good idea. Try to reference the problem you're solving for customers and your differentiation—those two together should make a knockout sales pitch.
- A **quick doodle** showing how it might look. Take note: I said a doodle, and I meant a doodle. Not a beautiful rendering or a final spec, just a back-of-the-napkin-style sketch to help everyone understand what you're talking about. Don't spend more than five minutes on it.

Approach summary

What it is (write the title of this approach)

Why it's a good idea (write one sentence)

How it might work (draw a quick doodle)

Here's how the "website + signs" summary might look for Genius Loci:

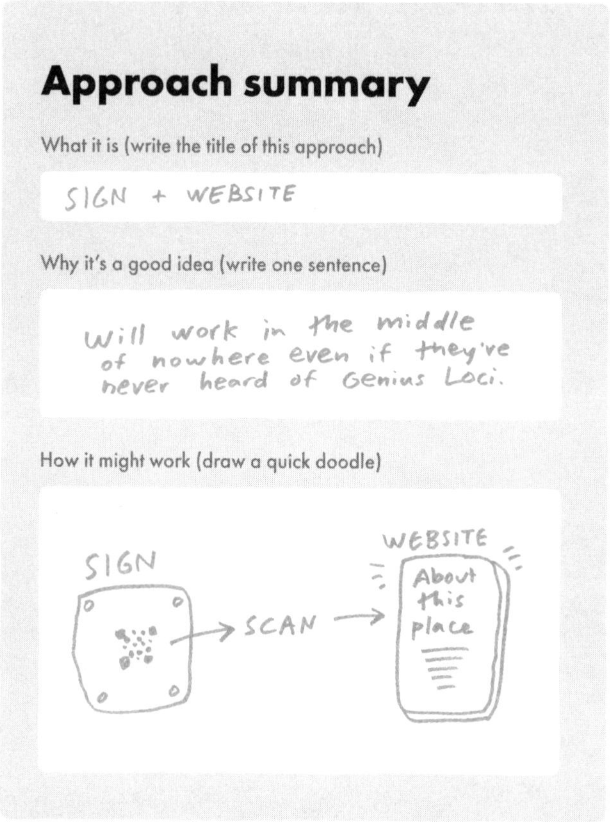

Once you've created these one-page summaries, you can be sure that every person has the same interpretation of each approach.

Making a choice among multiple options puts you in a strong position. Maybe, in the end, you'll go with your first idea, or maybe you'll go in a different direction, but either way, it will be a measured decision rather than a knee-jerk reaction. In the next chapter, I'll help you make that measured decision both carefully *and* quickly by using a neat visual trick.

8

Lenses

Around 2005, my dad bought a book called *Team of Rivals* by Doris Kearns Goodwin. *Team of Rivals* is a biography of Abraham Lincoln. It tells the story of how Lincoln battled political opponents William Seward, Edward Bates, and Salmon P. Chase, and how, when Lincoln was elected president, he invited all three of these rivals to become his advisors.

These guys had wildly different opinions about what the nation ought to do. They also weren't crazy about Lincoln, who defeated all three for the Republican presidential nomination. But Lincoln convinced them to join his cabinet, and throughout his presidency, Seward, Bates, and Chase challenged his ideas and offered competing perspectives. Before he committed to a course of action, Lincoln listened.

My dad loved *Team of Rivals*. He always valued contrary opinions, and when he learned Abraham Lincoln did, too? He was elated. Wouldn't stop talking about it. Year after year. Every phone call, every visit, every time I told him about my difficulties at work. "You know, Jake, Abraham Lincoln *sought out* the opinions of his opponents. Lincoln *listened*." "I know, Dad. I know!"

Slowly, very slowly, the idea began to sink in. I wanted to become a better leader. Could competing opinions help me make smarter decisions?

By this time, I was working at Google, and I began to follow my dad's advice. I started going out of my way to find contrary opinions. I forced myself to listen to the engineers *before* making a sales pitch for my own ideas. In meetings, I tried to list my colleagues' opinions on a whiteboard *before* making a decision. Sometimes I found that there was true consensus around one option. Sometimes I'd find one dissenting viewpoint that was so compelling I *had* to change my mind. Other times I'd hear the arguments and still decide to go with my own idea—but at least it was an informed decision.

Running this kind of "structured argument" felt awkward. But it worked. On the Gmail team, structured arguments helped me design a string of successful features. In Stockholm, structured arguments helped Serge, Mikael, and me make quick decisions to create the Google Meet prototype.

Eventually, JZ and I developed step-by-step recipes for structured arguments. The Note-and-Vote is the simplest and most versatile. The one I'm about to introduce, Magic Lenses, is the most powerful. All of them are based on the lesson I learned from my dad, with an assist from Abe Lincoln:

8. Consider conflicting opinions before you commit to an approach.

As usual, this lesson is easier said than done. Abraham Lincoln had a bunch of adversarial advisors and a high tolerance for heated

⑧

Consider conflicting opinions before you commit to an approach.

arguments, and if you have those, great—but most of us don't. Most of us work with like-minded teammates and most of us don't love to fight.

When we do disagree, it's hard to know how to handle it. Some common methods are playing devil's advocate (also known as "dishing out withering criticism but acting like you don't mean it"), passive-aggressive emails, and the ever-popular political dogfight. Since all of these are unpleasant, most of us keep our disagreements polite and brief. This kind of collegial environment is lovely—98 percent of the time.

But then there's that other 2 percent. The really big decisions. The kind of decision that dictates how we spend the other 98 percent of our time. When you're choosing how to approach a big project, you need to debate your options *without politics or personal bias* and you need to consider contrary opinions *even if those contrary opinions are not on your team.* You need Magic Lenses.

The next step in the Foundation Sprint is Magic Lenses. Magic Lenses are a visual representation of competing opinions. Instead of trying to hold different perspectives and arguments in your head, you can use Magic Lenses to *see* those perspectives, then analyze, compare, and make a quick decision.

To illustrate how Magic Lenses work, I'd like to briefly revisit the story of Genius Loci. As you may recall, Genius Loci generated several approaches to helping tourists find hidden gems. Let's focus on two of those: their first idea, an app with GPS, and the approach they chose in the end, a website and physical signs.

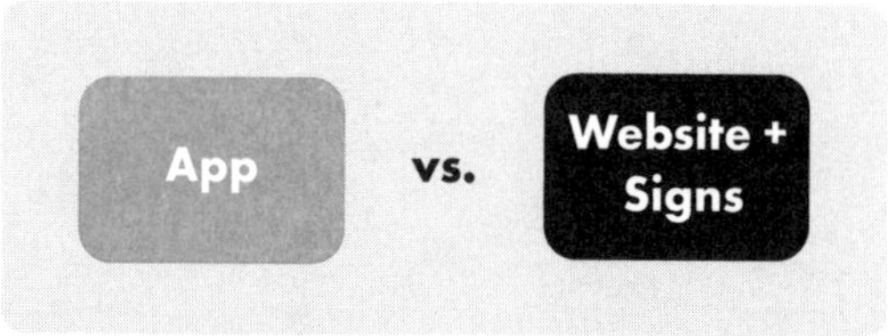

At the outset, Eglé and Stéph did *not* disagree with each other. They had the same vision: they wanted to make it super easy for tourists to discover stories about hidden points of interest, and they wanted to deliver those stories in the highest-quality interface. Seen through this "vision lens," they agreed that an app with GPS was the clear winner—it could use the phone's location to notify people when they got close to an interesting spot.

But that vision lens doesn't have to just be a mental construct. Let's make it visual, using a good old-fashioned 2x2 chart:

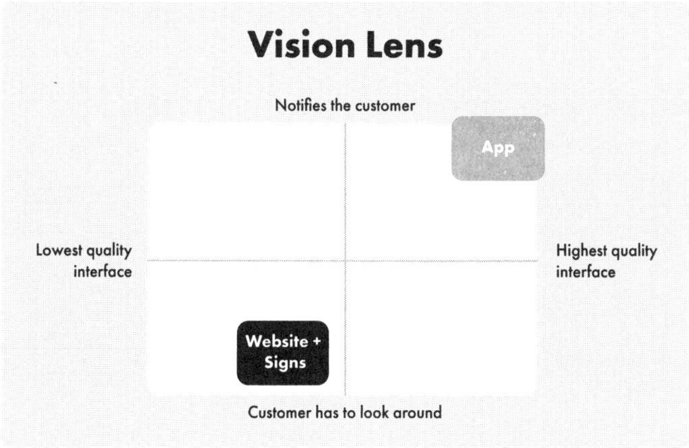

Even though they agreed on the vision, Eglé and Stéph resisted the urge to run with their first idea. They decided to have a debate—but since they didn't *actually* disagree with each other, they created a structured argument.

First, they tried to put themselves in the mindset of a stereotypical engineer. What would be the fastest, cheapest thing to build? They had to admit that an app would be expensive and slow. *Any* of the other options would be easier. Seen through this "pragmatic lens," the app doesn't look so great.

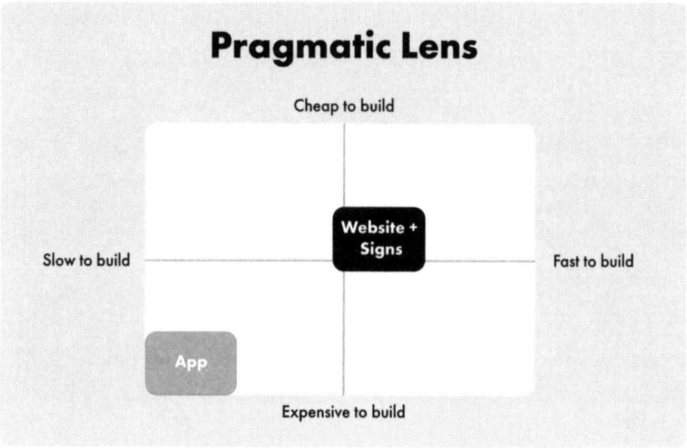

This new perspective gave them pause. Next, they thought about which approach would work best in the middle of nowhere. What if the cell signal was weak? What if the tourist had never heard of Genius Loci? In the "middle-of-nowhere lens," the app was once again a big loser.

How big a loser? It takes a 2x2 chart to really drive it home. The app is shoved into the lower left. Downtown Loserville.

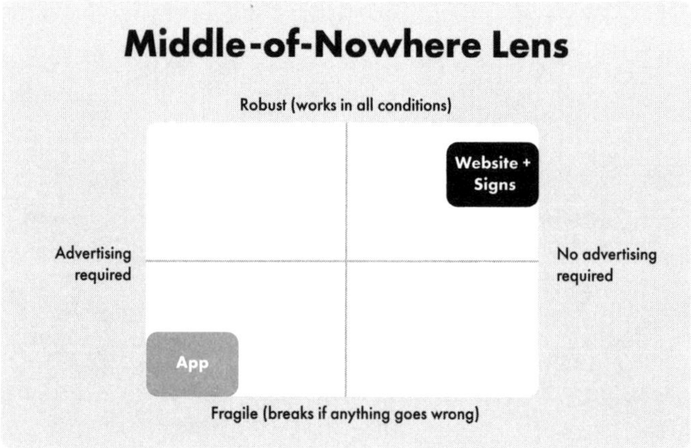

After considering the pragmatic lens and the middle-of-nowhere lens, Eglé and Stéph wondered if they had been too dismissive of the simpler options when they described a dream product. Were notifications *really* so magical? Plenty of phone notifications get ignored—a beautiful sign in a pristine location would be just as easy to find, if not easier. As for the interface, a website could be made to look an awful lot like an app.

Seen through this revised version of the vision lens, the combination of a website and physical signs appears to be an even better experience for tourists than the app.

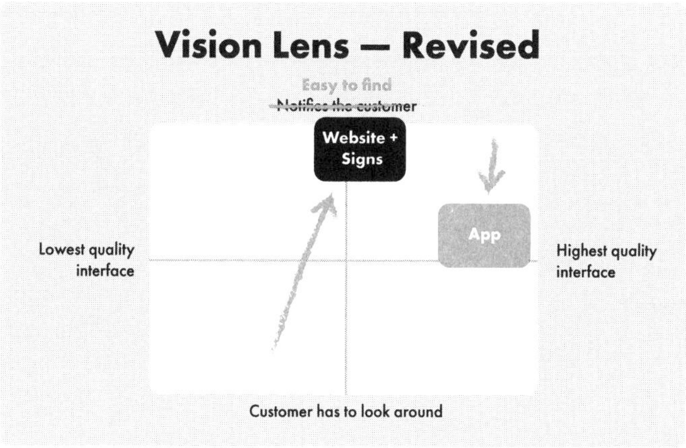

Now, all of this perspective switching? It's a *lot* of mental gymnastics. Examining a problem from different perspectives and weighing multiple options against multiple factors requires a huge amount of thinking. It strains the boundaries of our limited working memory. Just writing about it makes my forehead sweat.

That's why, yet again, the old 2x2 chart is so useful. It takes the complexity out of our heads and makes it visual. I'm telling you, 2x2 charts are underrated. And if we draw a series of charts as we go, we can then zoom out and look for patterns.

Considering these last three perspectives on Genius Loci—pragmatic, middle-of-nowhere, and revised vision lenses—the combination of website and signs is consistently strong. And in the crucial middle-of-nowhere lens, it wins by a mile. When we visualize the perspectives, the best approach is obvious.

That's how the Magic Lenses method works. It's an opportunity to turn a like-minded team into a team of rivals, to have a thorough argument without raising anyone's blood pressure, and to expand the capacity of our brains with the help of a simple visualization.

In practice, the Magic Lenses activity works a lot like the differentiation activity—but instead of one chart, you'll create several, and instead of competitors, you'll plot your own competing approaches. Here's how we do it:

Try the classic "team of rivals"

If I could give every team the perfect set of advisors, I'd include:

- A product visionary who imagines the dream solution for customers (**customer lens**)
- A pragmatic engineer who wants to build the product ASAP (**pragmatic lens**)
- A marketing wiz on a mission to make the business grow, grow, grow (**growth lens)**
- A finance expert intent on maximizing profit (**money lens**)

This list isn't random. In the hundreds of sprints JZ and I have run with companies, we've seen variations of these folks on many teams. These perspectives shake up the debate with new possibilities and priorities.

TEAM OF RIVALS
$
MONEY LENS
CUSTOMER LENS
DECIDER
GROWTH LENS
PRAGMATIC LENS

To illustrate how the classic "team of rivals" works, let's look at a Character portfolio company called Reclaim. Reclaim makes an AI-powered scheduling assistant—software that automatically organizes the customer's calendar to create time for focused work and reduce unnecessary meetings.

Reclaim wanted to make their AI more useful for their customers, and they had several ideas, but they weren't sure which was the best approach. So we ran a Foundation Sprint together to help them choose among these options:

- Synchronized "no meeting days" for teams
- Analytics to show how teams spend their time
- Smart scheduling links that understand your priorities

Here's how those different options look on the "team of rivals" charts:

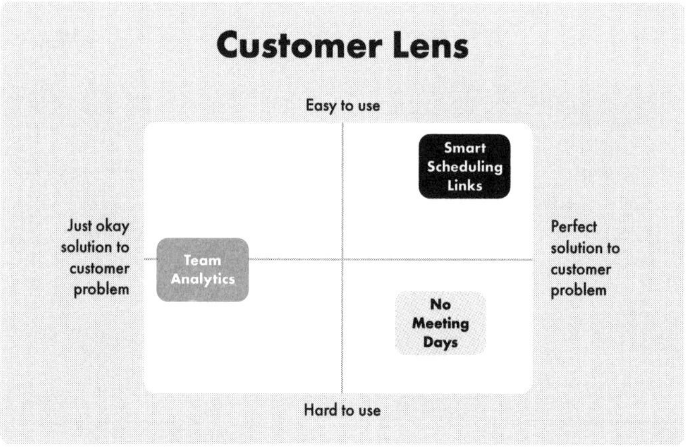

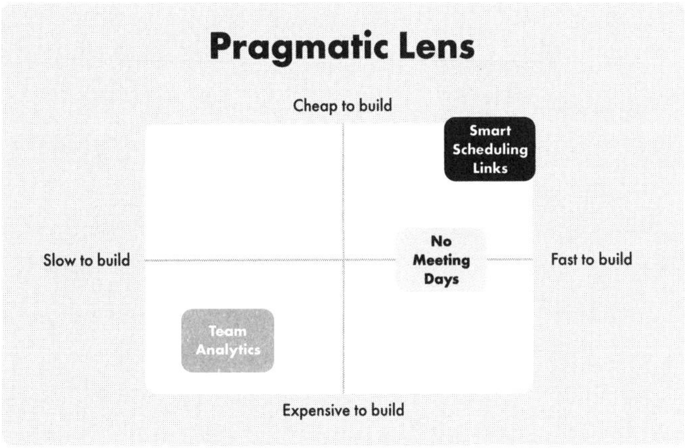
Pragmatic Lens
Cheap to build
Smart Scheduling Links
Slow to build
No Meeting Days
Fast to build
Team Analytics
Expensive to build

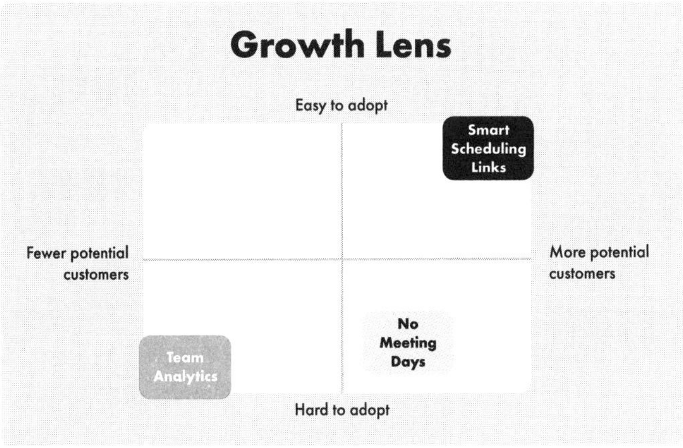
Growth Lens
Easy to adopt
Smart Scheduling Links
Fewer potential customers
More potential customers
No Meeting Days
Team Analytics
Hard to adopt

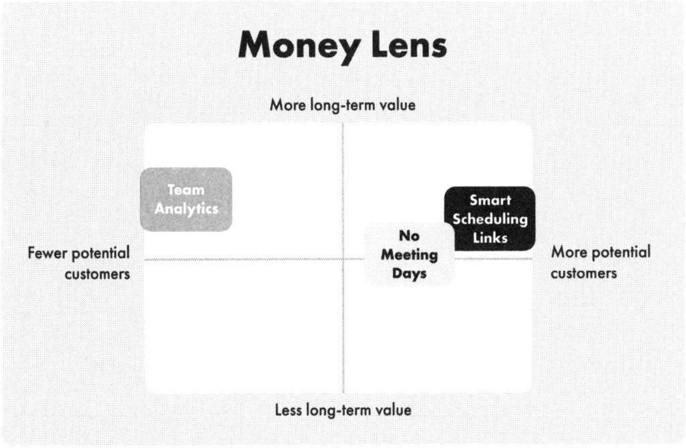
Money Lens
More long-term value
Team Analytics
Smart Scheduling Links
No Meeting Days
Fewer potential customers
More potential customers
Less long-term value

If you have a product visionary, pragmatic engineer, marketing wiz, and finance expert on your team, that's terrific. Let each one create his or her own chart.

But if you don't have a team of rivals, you can still do this exercise, with the charts substituting for the actual experts. No, it's not as good as the real thing—but it's a heck of a lot better than not considering alternate perspectives at all, which is what will happen otherwise.

Experts or not, you can use the default scales—"More long-term value" to "Less long-term value," "Easy to use" to "Hard to use," and so on—or you can choose your own factors based on what's important to your project. Just consider these a starting point.

Create custom lenses

Eglé and Stéph invented the middle-of-nowhere lens because it described a key risk to their project. You, too, should go beyond the "team of rivals" and create custom lenses. You can use any criteria that are important to your project's success.

In their Foundation Sprint, Reclaim's founders wanted to choose an approach that would "cure pain" for their customers, that is, alleviate the stress people felt when managing their calendars. They also wanted an approach for which customers would be happy to pay. So they created a "Revenue + Cure" lens.

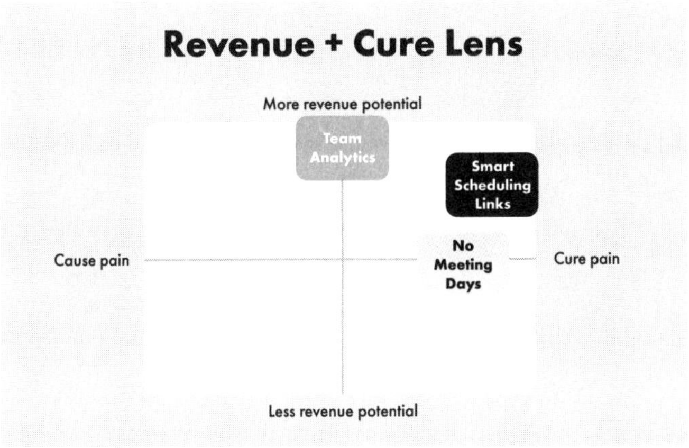

Most teams find it useful to create anywhere from one to three of these custom lenses. You can also use your differentiation chart (from chapter 5) as a lens. The idea is simply to expand the number of perspectives you consider before you decide.

Zoom out, review, and decide

Finally, zoom out and look at all of your 2x2 charts. You'll be able to see which colors (or letters) score in the top right of each chart. Patterns will emerge.

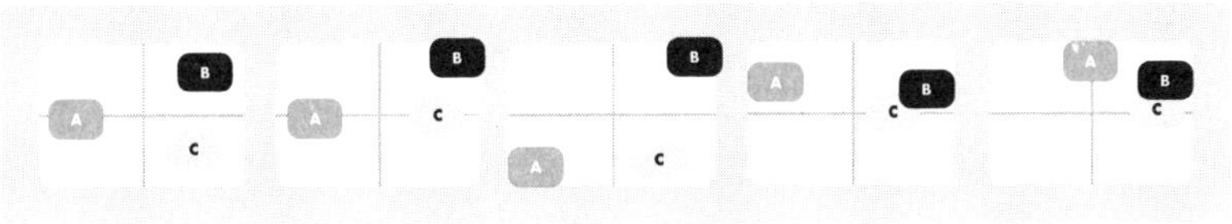

Sometimes, there is consensus: the same option wins in most lenses or even in all of them. Sometimes, when you review everything, one lens stands out as the right way to evaluate the project. Either way, at this point, it's time for the Decider to decide on an approach. Choose one option to be your top bet (your first choice approach) and one as a backup (the first option to consider if you need to pivot).

For Reclaim, the pattern was clear. "Smart Scheduling Links" (option B) consistently appeared in the top right of every Magic Lens. What was interesting was that, coming into their Foundation Sprint, *nobody* on the Reclaim team thought Smart Scheduling Links would be the best approach to take. Magic Lenses changed their minds.

Reclaim launched Smart Scheduling Links in April 2023. Customers loved it, and it became the startup's fastest-growing feature, with thousands of people adopting it each month. Meanwhile, Reclaim continued to revisit their 2x2 charts, building features that scored in the top right. By early 2024, their software was being used by more than 300,000 people at more than 40,000 companies and, in July 2024, Reclaim was acquired by Dropbox.

Running the Magic Lenses exercise allows your team to stop mentally juggling everything at once—all of the factors and options and arguments—and frees up precious mental resources that you can marshal for making a good decision.

Day two of the Foundation Sprint is almost over, but there is one more important step. Because even after all of today's analysis, all you have are your opinions—and if there's one thing I've learned from watching BBC's *Pride and Prejudice* seventeen times, it's that first opinions are not to be trusted.

In the next chapter, I'll show you how to forge your opinions into a Founding Hypothesis that you can test. I'll also tell you a story about how even the most brilliant mind can latch on to the wrong idea—and never let it go.

Tiny Loops

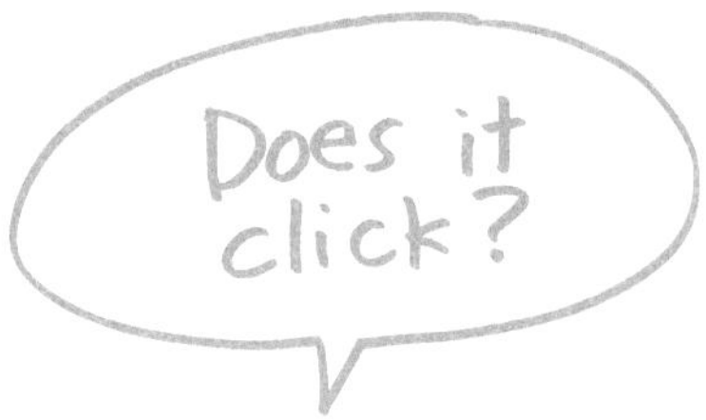
Does it click?

A strategy is just a **hypothesis**.

Run **experiments**, establish confidence,

and then build a product that clicks.

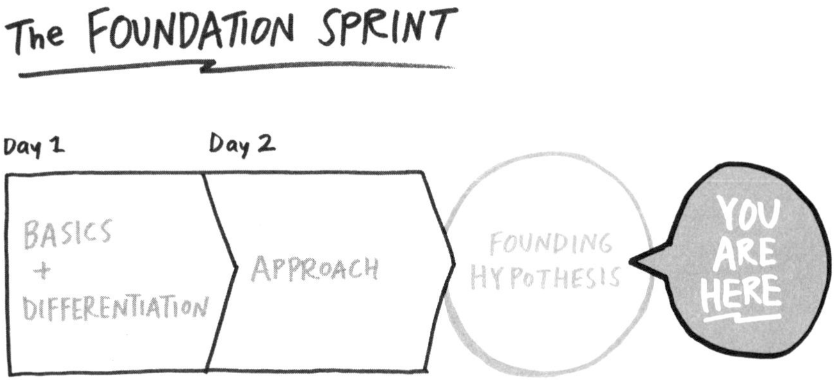
The FOUNDATION SPRINT
Day 1
Day 2
BASICS + DIFFERENTIATION
APPROACH
FOUNDING HYPOTHESIS
YOU ARE HERE

9

Hypothesis

On September 23, 1846, an assistant at the Berlin Observatory received a letter. He opened it. He read it. His eyes probably got big, and he probably reread it while murmuring excitedly to himself in German. I'm making up his reaction, but this next part definitely happened: That evening, following the letter's instructions, the assistant pointed the observatory's telescope at a precise point in the night sky. He peered through the eyepiece. And there it was. A previously undiscovered object: the planet Neptune.

The author of the mystery letter was a French guy named Urbain Le Verrier. Le Verrier was a math genius. He studied irregularities in the orbit of Uranus and, in accordance with Isaac Newton's laws of motion, predicted that there was an eighth planet causing the disruptions. He calculated exactly where this hypothetical planet would be on any given night. He needed a professional astronomer with a powerful telescope to prove his prediction, so he sent the letter to Berlin.

Discovering Neptune must have felt fantastic, and afterward, Le Verrier became a big deal in scientific circles. You probably couldn't have a happening French mathematics party if you didn't at least *try* to get Le Verrier to show up—but good luck with that, because he was already busy with a new project.

Throughout the rest of the 1840s and into the 1850s, Le Verrier used his number-crunching prowess to calculate the precise orbits of all the other planets in the solar system. Then, in 1859, he dropped another bombshell on the astronomy world: his calculations revealed new orbital irregularities pointing to the existence of a *ninth* planet.

Nope, not Pluto. Le Verrier predicted that this ninth planet, which he called Vulcan, could be found between the sun and Mercury. Around the world, astronomers followed Le Verrier's instructions, pointed their telescopes at the sun—seriously, do NOT try that at home—and searched for Vulcan.

Nothing.

Then an amateur astronomer spotted a tiny dot moving across the sun. Le Verrier investigated and announced that he'd found proof of Vulcan. The press went wild. But no professionals could verify the amateur's observation. Then another amateur spotted something, and Le Verrier kicked off another wave of excitement, but this data also could not be corroborated. This happened again. And again. For the next eighteen years, amateur astronomers looked for Vulcan, and sometimes they saw . . . something? A sunspot? A planet? Each time, Le Verrier announced that Vulcan had finally been discovered. Each time, no reputable astronomer could verify the data. No matter how often he was proved wrong, Le Verrier refused to let go of his hypothesis. He searched in vain for Vulcan until his death in 1877.

There is no planet Vulcan.* In 1916, Albert Einstein solved the

*Which is a bummer, because Vulcan is such a great name. So is Neptune, for that matter—it's too bad Le Verrier didn't get to name Uranus.

mystery of Mercury's irregular orbit with his theory of relativity: Apparently, the sun is so massive that it bends space-time and *that* is what warps Mercury's orbit. Le Verrier's math was correct, but his desire to discover another planet blinded him from something even more astonishing: there is more to the universe than Newton's laws.

Le Verrier was doing what scientists do: stare into the unknown, make predictions, and run experiments. Sometimes the experiment works and the scientist is a hero—but more often, the prediction is incorrect. Heck, even Einstein got things wrong. In 1917, he declared that the universe is static; then, in 1929, Edwin Hubble proved that the universe is expanding.*

But there is a key difference between Einstein and Le Verrier. When Einstein was proven wrong, he acknowledged the error—which he called his "biggest blunder"—and adjusted his equations. He changed his worldview.

Le Verrier, on the other hand, spent eighteen years with tunnel vision on Vulcan. What if he had acknowledged that his planet hypothesis was wrong and moved on? I'm not suggesting that he would have come up with the theory of relativity, but he could have, I don't know, worked on a different project? With his rare analytical skills, Le Verrier might have made another truly worthwhile contribution to mankind, like inventing Wordle. We'll never know.

So what, exactly, was Le Verrier's problem?

Well, he was only human.

Researchers have identified patterns of mistakes that humans make, again and again, when confronted with complex situations. Our

*The condensed details: Edwin Hubble proved that the universe is expanding by combining his own research with Henrietta Swan Leavitt's model for measuring vast distances and Vesto Slipher's discovery that distant galaxies are redshifted. And man, how great must it have felt to prove Einstein wrong? In your face, Albert!

poor brains want to conserve energy, so they take shortcuts—and they take shortcuts in predictable ways that lead to predictable errors.

These predictable errors are called cognitive biases. According to those researchers, there are over 180 cognitive biases, but for my money, these are the greatest hits:

- **Anchoring bias:** Falling in love with the first option
- **Self-serving bias:** Favoring an approach that promotes our self-interest and ego
- **Overconfidence bias:** Believing positive assumptions and ignoring risk
- **Confirmation bias:** Seeking only data that confirms our belief

Le Verrier fell prey to all four of these biases. When he discovered Mercury's orbital anomaly, his first explanation was, understandably, that it was a new planet. But he became obsessed with that first explanation (anchoring bias). He became even more committed as he imagined the accolades of discovering a new planet for the *second* time (self-serving bias). He was certain his explanation was correct (overconfidence bias), so he put his faith in questionable data that supported what he wanted to be true (confirmation bias).

Cognitive biases exert a powerful influence—and not only on nineteenth-century French mathematicians, but also on modern-day startup founders, business leaders, executives, and, well, all of us. These biases work together like a pack of wolves: anchoring bias grabs us by the collar, then self-serving, overconfidence, and confirmation biases all pile on. They push us—hard—to lock in on one option without analyzing the alternatives. And they're invisible: once we're under their sway, we don't feel biased, we feel conviction.

But these biases can be overcome. All you have to do is use a little science.

• • •

At the end of the Foundation Sprint, you're like a scientist staring into the unknown. You have a formula—in your case, a project approach and differentiation—and a prediction: that people will want what you make. It's all very logical. But as you move forward, I want you to be like Einstein, not Le Verrier.

See, until your solution clicks with customers, your whole foundation is just an educated guess. And I hate to say it, but in one way or another, that guess is almost certainly wrong. Maybe you're taking the wrong approach. Maybe you're differentiating on speed when people care most about simplicity. Maybe you chose the wrong problem or the wrong customer. First guesses might be off by a lot or a little—but they are almost always off. To put it another way:

9. It's just a hypothesis until you prove it.

So don't call your foundation a *plan* just yet. A plan is a commitment. With a plan, it's easy to feel—as Le Verrier probably felt—that if you're wrong, your reputation is at stake.

A hypothesis, on the other hand? That's just a guess. It should feel fluid and flexible. A hypothesis is intended to be tested, proven wrong, and updated. It's a tool for learning.

We designed the Foundation Sprint to get you started fast so you can *learn* fast, not so you can *commit* fast. The final step in the Foundation Sprint is to condense all of your fundamental guesses into a Founding Hypothesis.

⑨

It's just a hypothesis until you prove it.

Just fill in the blanks in this sentence:

Founding Hypothesis

If we help	customer
solve	problem
with	approach
they will choose it over	competitors
because our solution is	differentiation

For example, here's the Founding Hypothesis for the game I made in high school:

Mealy Mouse

Founding Hypothesis

If I help	**high schoolers**
solve	**boredom**
with	**a maze game**
they will choose it over	**corn dogs & exercise**
because my solution is	**fast & humiliating**

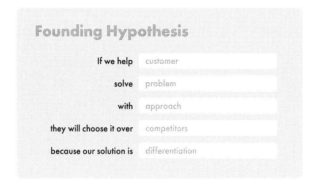

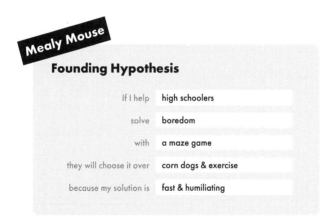

Here are a couple more:

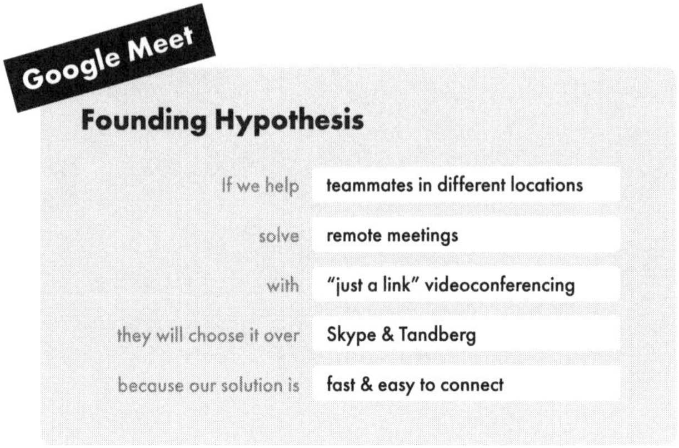
Google Meet
Founding Hypothesis
If we help
teammates in different locations
solve
remote meetings
with
"just a link" videoconferencing
they will choose it over
Skype & Tandberg
because our solution is
fast & easy to connect

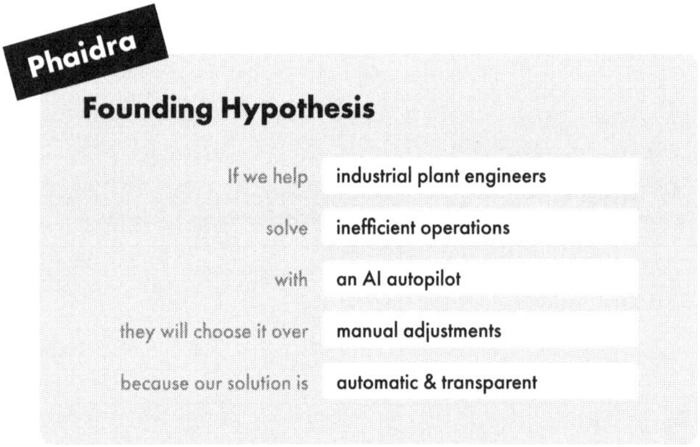
Phaidra
Founding Hypothesis
If we help
industrial plant engineers
solve
inefficient operations
with
an AI autopilot
they will choose it over
manual adjustments
because our solution is
automatic & transparent

Every big project is full of predictions, but they normally remain hidden behind the scenes. With the Founding Hypothesis, you pull those predictions onto center stage, and hit them with a dazzling spotlight. And you might not like what you see. For example, imagine the Founding Hypothesis for the Skyscraper Robot from the movie *Big*. In this case, the Founding Hypothesis acts like Tom Hanks, pointing out the absurdity of the project's premise. But even if your foundation is rational, plainly stating your predictions can be startling.

Skyscraper Robot

Founding Hypothesis

If we help	kids
solve	play
with	a toy building
they will choose it over	G.I. Joe, LEGO, and Nintendo
because our solution is	architectural & motionless

When Stéph Cruchon, Genius Loci's cofounder, looked at their Founding Hypothesis for the first time, he was taken aback. "When I saw it all in one place, it was like, *Oh my god, we have to beat Apple AND Google!?* But then I thought, this isn't so crazy. They aren't trying to solve undiscovered local stories, so if people care about that, we have a chance to win."

Genius Loci

Founding Hypothesis

If we help	travelers
solve	discovering local stories
with	physical signs + a website
they will choose it over	Google Maps & Apple Maps
because our solution is	rich & story-filled

Every time I look at a Founding Hypothesis, I think, "Prove it!" Each prediction in the Founding Hypothesis lends itself to an existential, testable question about the project.

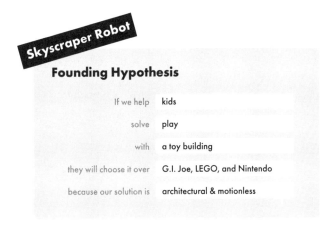

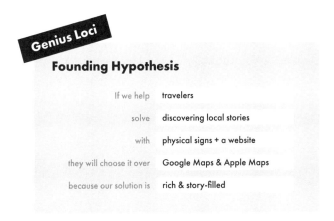

To make these questions plain, JZ and I give teams a scorecard that adds a question to each prediction: Do you have the right customer? Right problem? Right approach? Will people *really* choose your solution over the competition? Do they care about your chosen differentiators, and will they believe your solution is radically better when judged by those criteria? And of course, above all: Does it click?

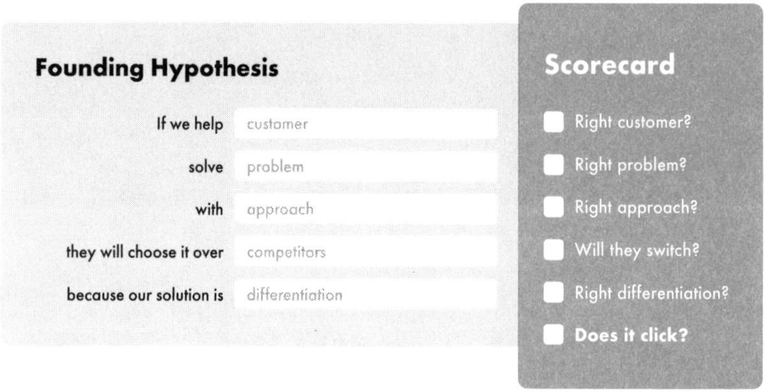
Founding Hypothesis
If we help
customer
solve
problem
with
approach
they will choose it over
competitors
because our solution is
differentiation
Scorecard
Right customer?
Right problem?
Right approach?
Will they switch?
Right differentiation?
Does it click?

These are essential questions. They force us to assess whether we're doing work that matters. They force our gaze away from just *what* we're building toward *who* we're building it for: our customers.

If you were doing things the old way, you'd have to build and launch a finished product before you answered these questions. That's pretty freaking frightening, and it's why most teams prefer to ignore their underlying predictions.

But you don't have to fear your predictions. You can face them immediately. Imagine if Urbain Le Verrier had access to the *Millennium Falcon*: he could've just zoomed around the solar system to see what was up. Well, that's you. The Foundation Sprint is complete, but your experiments have just begun. In the next chapter, I'll show you how Phaidra used tiny loops to test and adjust their solution and prove their Founding Hypothesis—and how you can do the same.

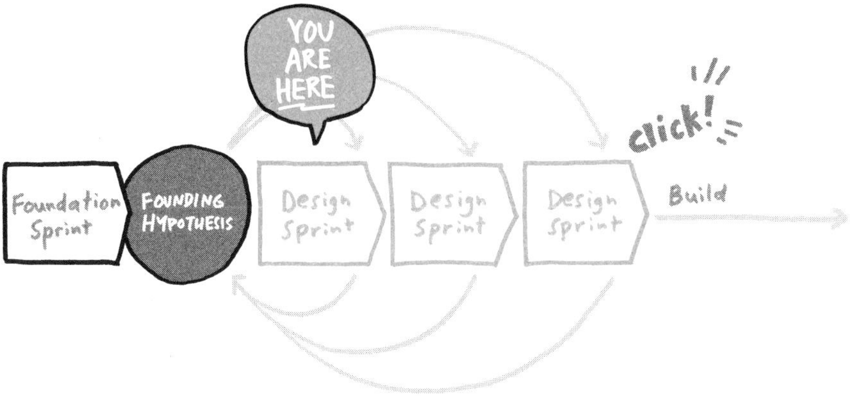

YOU ARE HERE
Click!
Foundation Sprint
FOUNDING HYPOTHESIS
Design Sprint
Design Sprint
Design Sprint
Build

10

Experiment

There was one convenience store in the small town where I grew up: a place called Con's Pitstop. In the front of Con's they sold penny candy; in the back were a couple of coin-operated arcade games, and in 1987, one of those games was *Super Mario Bros.*

I'll never forget the first time I tried it. My friend Sean loaned me a quarter and gave me an overview of the controls: push the A button to jump, the B button to run. I waited and waited in line. Finally, it was my turn. Kids were watching. My hands were sweaty. On my first attempt, I got the buttons confused and killed Mario by running him straight into a Goomba—a waddling mushroom, the easiest enemy in the game. Embarrassing. On my second attempt, it happened *again*. Kids laughed. My pulse pounded in my ears. On my third and final try, I jumped to evade the marching mushroom, hit Mario's head on a brick, fell straight back to earth, and . . . was once again killed by the Goomba. Game over.

I tried *Super Mario Bros.* a few more times at Con's, on those rare occasions I was in town with a quarter in my pocket. Every time, there was a crowd, and every time, I was terrible. But I wanted to figure it out. So I saved money from mowing the lawn, picking up rocks in our field, and my allowance, and once I had enough, I bought a Nintendo Entertainment System. And then I got to try *Super Mario Bros.* at home. It was a totally different experience.

On the coin-op machine at Con's, opportunities were scarce, everyone was watching, and twenty-five cents were on the line for each attempt. It was super stressful.

On my Nintendo at home, I could try over and over. There was no penalty for failure and no big audience. As a result, I wasn't tense, I was *playing*. I experimented, learned, and improved until I could make it all the way to the end and defeat the big boss, Bowser—not every time, but sometimes. I could even play at Con's without getting laughed out of the building, and it wasn't an ordeal. It was fun.

Big projects can be stressful. They cost lots of time and money and, in most cases, you only have one opportunity to get it right. In this chapter, I'll show you how to create unlimited chances, so that, like a 1980s kid with a Nintendo, you can practice until you master the challenge. To show you how it works, let's pick up the story of Phaidra, the startup building AI for factories and industrial plants.

As we rejoin Katie, Jim, and Veda, the three have left their old jobs, founded their new company, raised money, and hired a small team of elite engineers and product experts.

Phaidra was at the beginning of a big project. They planned to create an AI "autopilot" for industrial plants: software that could autonomously monitor sensors and adjust controls, freeing the engineers who ran those plants for more important (and more interesting) duties. Building this software would be challenging enough, but they also had to convince the engineers that the AI would make good decisions. As Katie put it, "It doesn't matter how good the technology is if our customers don't understand it or trust it."

Phaidra

Founding Hypothesis

If we help	industrial plant engineers
solve	inefficient operations
with	an AI autopilot
they will choose it over	manual adjustments
because our solution is	automatic & transparent

Phaidra figured they could establish that trust through transparency: showing engineers what the AI was doing and why. But in the beginning, it was all just a hypothesis. What should the product look like, and how should it work? The normal order of operations would be for Phaidra to form a plan, build a solution, and then, maybe a year or two later, sell it to customers and find out if their hypothesis was correct. Instead, they tested their hypothesis immediately by working in sprints.

First, they cleared their calendars for a full week. They scheduled interviews with plant engineers for Friday of that week, creating a tight deadline for themselves. Then they set to work designing a prototype.

On Monday, they mapped out how plant engineers would hear about Phaidra's product, how they would start using it, and how they would interact with it day-to-day. The Phaidra team couldn't prototype everything in one week—it was far too complex. So Katie, acting as Decider (the decision-maker in a sprint; see chapter 1), chose to focus on what she believed was the most crucial element: the AI dashboard. This dashboard would have to humanize the synthetic thought process of the AI so that engineers could assess whether the autopilot was making good decisions. If it was clear and helpful, the dashboard could be the key selling point for engineers—but if it was confusing, it could be an instant deal-breaker.

On Tuesday, the Phaidra team sketched proposals for the dashboard design. In Vancouver, British Columbia, Veda drew a series of rectangles on a blank sheet of paper. He added details: a temperature chart here, a list of messages there, an expandable panel on the side. A schematic took form with each stroke of ink.

A few hundred miles south, in Hood Canal, Washington, Katie Hoffman and Jim Gao worked in separate rooms, each designing schematics of their own. Meanwhile, around the country, the rest of the Phaidra team—Christopher Vause, Mandi Fong, Christine Phillips, and Paritosh Mohan—worked alone on sketches. In Milwaukee, John

Jim Gao sketching a proposal for the Phaidra dashboard.

John Zeratsky sketching a proposal for the Phaidra dashboard.

Zeratsky referred to his notes, then began filling in a page of his own. (JZ and I got to join in on these sprints.)

By the end of the day, the team had nine competing proposals, each detailing a different way that the dashboard could work.

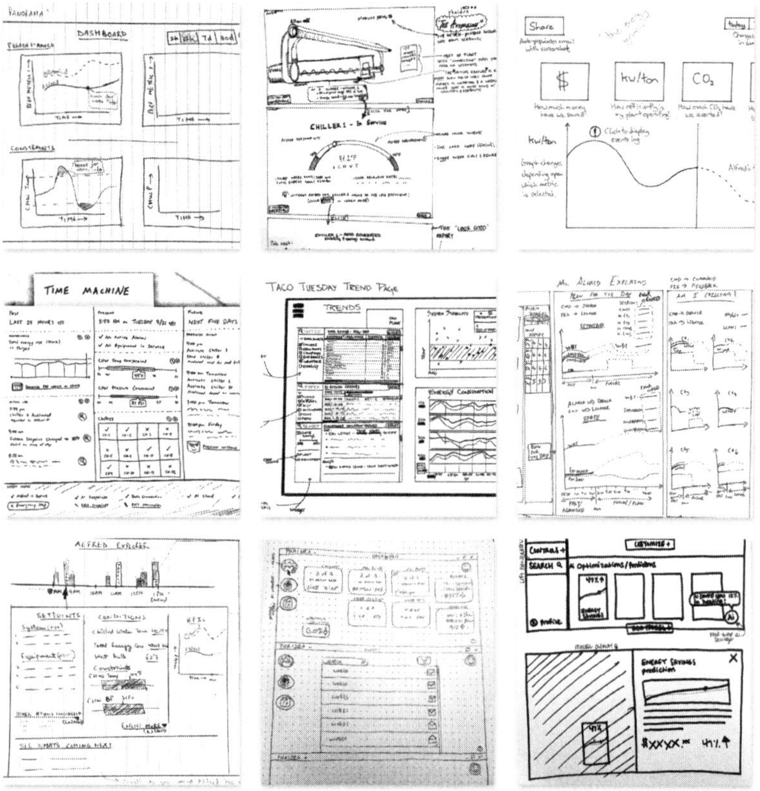

On Wednesday, continuing to "work alone together," the team reviewed the proposals and voted in silence. Then they held a structured debate, and Katie chose which solutions she wanted to test with customers.

On Thursday, the last day before their interviews with plant engineers, the team turned the winning sketches into a prototype. This prototype wasn't functional. Instead, it was a realistic fake: a series of mock-ups linked together to simulate how the dashboard would work once the autopilot software was complete.

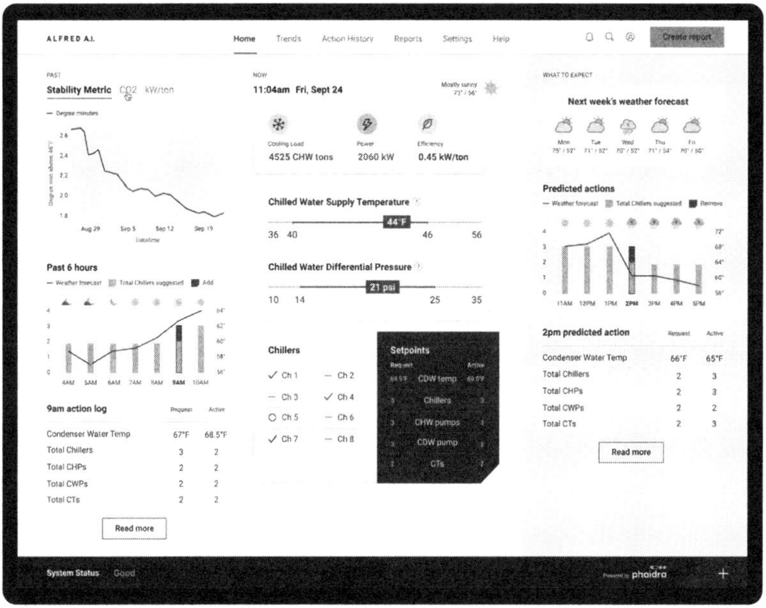

Then, on Friday, they interviewed four plant engineers in four separate Zoom calls. In each call, the Phaidra team asked the engineers about their work, then watched as the engineer tried to use the dashboard, make sense of the autopilot, and, finally, consider whether to sign up their plant for a trial run of the software. Remember, at this point the autopilot software didn't actually exist—but Phaidra used the "sign-up" question to assess whether engineers had sincere interest.

The engineers were *not* interested.

That prototype the Phaidra team sweated over all week? It just wasn't good enough. The dashboard design didn't show sufficient detail, so the engineers couldn't understand how the autopilot was making its decisions. Two of the engineers were somewhat skeptical of Phaidra's product. The other two were *very* skeptical. Nobody was ready to sign up.

But as Katie and the Phaidra team considered the key elements of their hypothesis, they saw reason for optimism. Were these the right customers? Yes; these engineers had the power to block Phaidra's AI from their plants if they didn't believe in it. Was Phaidra tackling the right problem? Again, yes: inefficient operations worried these plant engineers, and manual monitoring and adjusting was a tedious hassle. The AI autopilot still looked like the right approach.

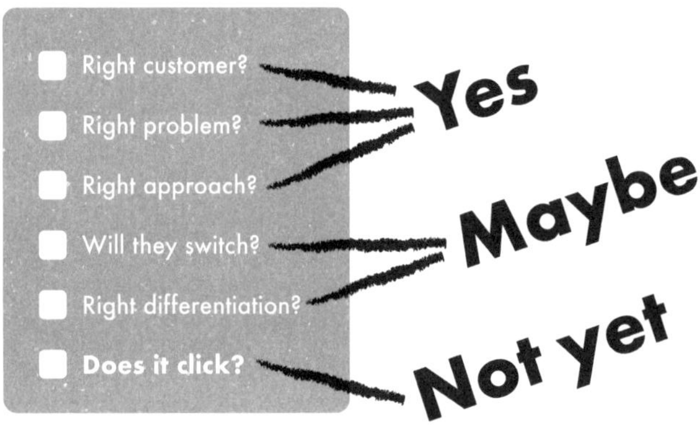

The problem was that Phaidra hadn't yet delivered on their differentiation. The dashboard promised to automatically run the plant—which engineers liked—but it wasn't transparent enough to build trust in the autopilot software. Yet.

Now that they had seen their first solution fail, however, the team had lots of ideas about how to make it better. So they cleared the calendar for the next week and did it all over again. They sketched a new slate of proposed solutions. They reviewed the proposals and chose a new approach. They built a new prototype. The next Friday, they tested with four more engineers.

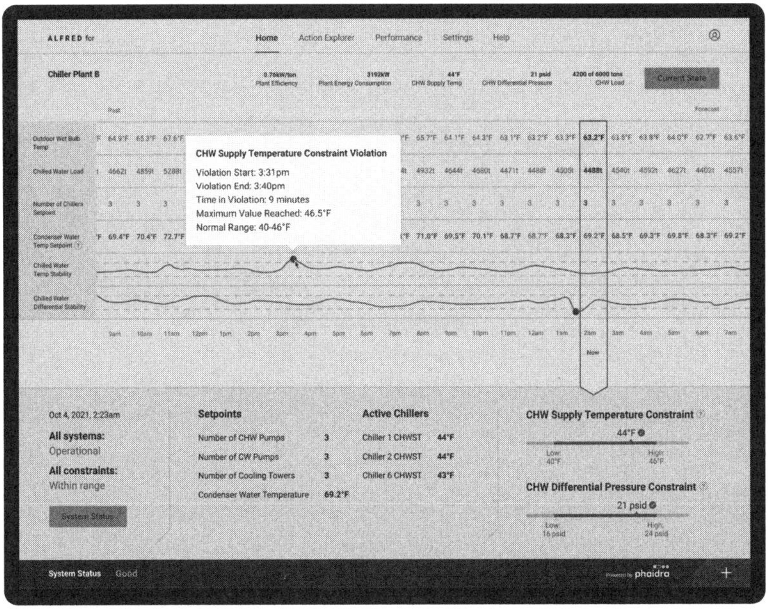

This new dashboard was *full* of details. It featured a big timeline showing the autopilot's actions from the past day alongside its forecast for the next few hours, and you could tap anywhere for nitty-gritty specifics about each decision and adjustment.

In the interviews, the engineers started out skeptical. But as they examined the timeline and scrutinized the details, they started to nod their heads. By the end of the interviews, they were ready to sign up their plants for a test run with the real AI.

Katie, Jim, Veda, and the rest of the Phaidra team were elated. They had upended their careers in their quest to make industrial plants more efficient. Now they had seen the autopilot click—and their vision felt within reach.

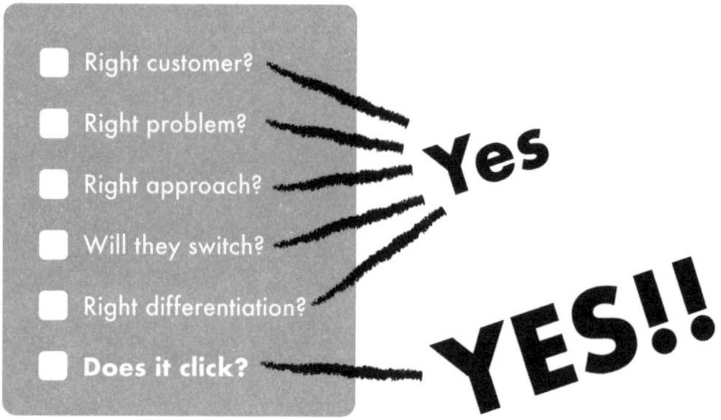

Let's take a look at what just happened. Phaidra had a Founding Hypothesis. Instead of doing things the normal way—spending months planning and executing before putting their product in front of customers—they started with short, focused bursts. There is one more lesson here:

10. Experiment with tiny loops until your solution clicks. Then build it.

At the beginning of this book, I told a story about the video game I made in high school. Every week, I tried a new unfinished game with my friends, creating a "tiny loop" between my hypothesis and my customers.

⑩

Experiment with tiny loops until your solution clicks. Then build it.

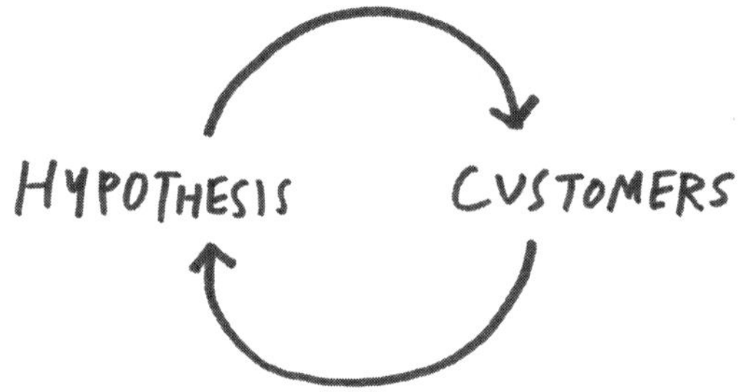

Phaidra did the same thing by testing prototypes before their software existed. These tiny loops gave Katie, Jim, and Veda as many attempts as they needed to make their solution click *before* making the high-stakes decision to build. They were playing Nintendo at home to master the game.

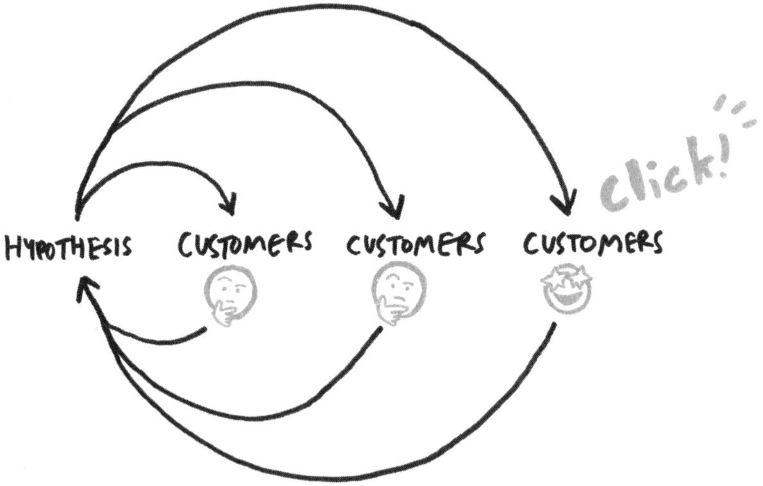

Tiny loops are essential for ambitious projects because it takes *so long* to launch a product and get real-world data. How long, exactly? Well, that depends.

Maybe you work in a big organization or you're creating a physical product. Early in my career, when I was at Microsoft, we used to sell software on CD-ROMs—shiny silver platters filled with data. By the time we got multiple teams to agree to a plan, then wrote code, manufactured the CD-ROMs, put them in boxes, shipped them to stores, and waited for sales reports, it took *over a year* to get real-world data. That's a long loop.

But maybe your team moves a bit faster. When I went to work at Google in the mid-2000s, the typical project timeline was only three months. It was exhilarating . . . until I realized that, although the *plan* was three months, the *reality* was that building and fixing and tweaking and preparing and launching took us a year. Or more. Every time. That's another long loop.

But maybe you're moving at startup speed. Startups must find "product-market fit"—that is, a market of people who will pay for their product—before they run out of money. So, instead of a perfect solution, most startups build a simpler product that is just enough to be useful to customers, and launch it as quickly as possible. This is called a "minimum viable product" or MVP, and it's a smart tactic for moving fast.

How fast can startups go? New tools keep appearing, promising to speed things up—the latest being artificial intelligence—but instead of launching faster, founders just make their MVPs more ambitious. They plan to be done in a few weeks, but building even a stripped-down version of an ambitious solution takes time, and of course, ambitious founders have high standards, and they know customers have high expectations, so making sure it's *really* ready takes *even more* time, and then they have to figure out how to explain this new thing to those customers and . . . before you know it, it takes a year. Even MVPs are a long loop.

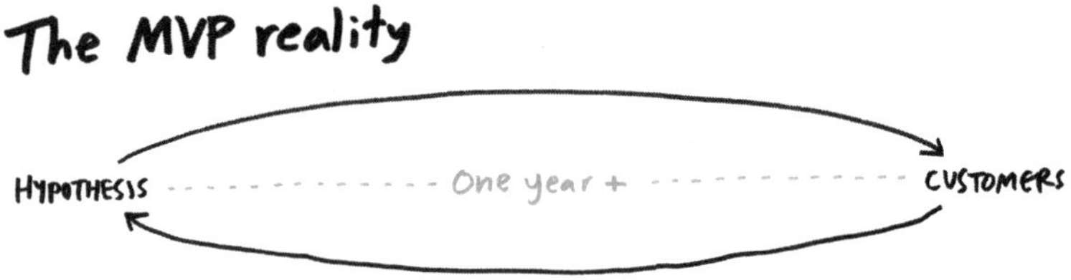

There is a pattern here. So, in the tradition of Isaac Newton, I humbly offer you Jake's Laws of Project Motion:

1. Ambitious projects take at least a year.
2. Or twice as long as planned.
3. Whichever is greater.

In my experience, this is true (pretty much) everywhere. I'm not saying MVPs are a bad idea—far from it. I'm not saying teams should stop being ambitious or build slipshod products to save time—please don't. I'm just saying that, if you want to make a great solution to a real problem, it will probably take at least twelve months, and since that is *way* too long to wait to test your hypothesis, you need tiny loops.

There are many ways to run tiny loops, but I recommend the week-long technique that Phaidra used. It's called the Design Sprint. As you might recall from earlier in the book, the Design Sprint is the five-day process I created at Google to help teams solve problems and test new ideas. It works like this:

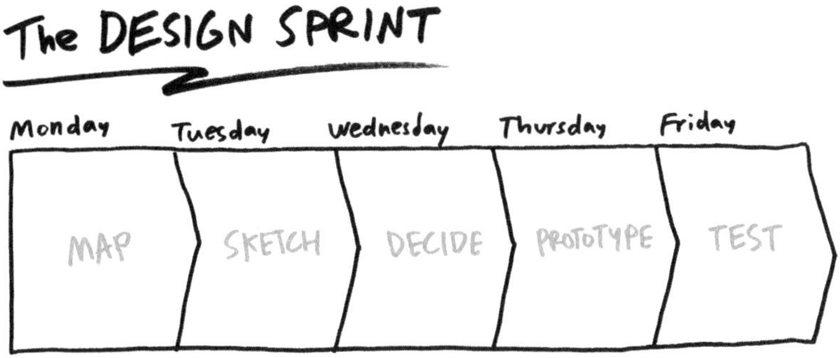

- On Monday, **map** out the customer problem.
- On Tuesday, **sketch** competing solutions on paper.
- On Wednesday, **decide** which solutions to test.
- On Thursday, create realistic **prototypes**.
- On Friday, **test** with customers.

So far in this book, you've learned how to compress months of debate into the first two days of your project with the Foundation Sprint. The Design Sprint offers another kind of calendar distortion: a time machine that zooms you into the future so you can see how customers react *before* you build your solution.

JZ and I use the Design Sprint all the time in our work at Character Capital. It's the perfect follow-up to the Foundation Sprint. Yes, clearing your team's calendar for a week at a time can feel extreme, but when placed on a year-plus timeline, two days for a Foundation Sprint plus another five days for each Design Sprint doesn't look so big.

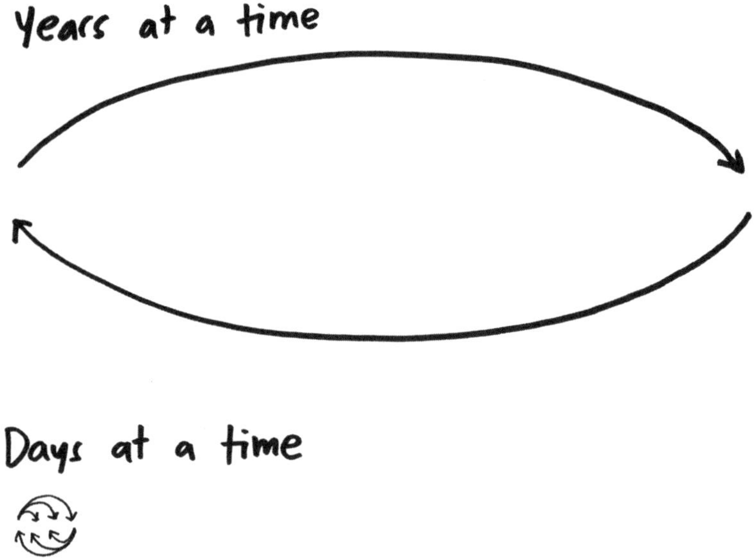

When MVPs fail to find product-market fit, pivoting takes months. When prototypes don't click with customers, you can adjust in hours. So, as far as JZ and I are concerned, spending a few days up front to align your team and de-risk your project is a very smart investment.

If you'd like to use Design Sprints to run those experiments, here are some tips to get you started:

Follow the checklist

You don't have to make up the Design Sprint as you go along—we've got a proven step-by-step plan to take you from Monday morning to Friday afternoon. Our book *Sprint* is a complete guide to the process, and you can also find a guide with videos on thesprintbook.com. Tens of thousands of teams around the world have run their own Design Sprints, and you can, too.

You can prototype anything

The Design Sprint is not just for software—the process is flexible enough to help with all kinds of projects. We use the same five-day recipe to prototype and test sales decks, marketing materials, advertising, software, physical devices, in-person services, printed medical reports, process changes for organizations . . . the list goes on.

Focus on risks

Make a list of the most important risks to your project, then use the Design Sprint to dig in and defuse them. The question "Can we build trust?" was at the top of Phaidra's risk list (as it is for many big projects), so that's where Katie focused their prototypes and tests.

Prove the story first

In your first Design Sprint, consider focusing on how customers will discover your product, learn about it, and decide whether to try it for the first time. Whether it's a sales deck or a marketing website, testing your product's story gives you a chance to assess many of the key questions on your scorecard: Are you talking to the right customers? Do they have the problem you think they have? Does your differentiation appeal to them?

Not only that, but prototyping a sales deck or marketing website is almost certainly easier than prototyping software, physical products, services, or whatever your solution might be. A few mock-up images of the finished product might be enough to determine whether your customers are willing to take the next step—and that means you can spend some extra time creating competing prototypes.

Test multiple prototypes head-to-head

The biggest advantage of Design Sprints over MVPs is that you can try multiple solutions at once. Teams never create multiple MVPs—it's just too time-consuming—but in a Design Sprint, you can turbocharge your learning by creating and testing more than one prototype head-to-head.

In our book *Sprint*, we wrote about how Slack used Design Sprints in 2015, with CEO Stewart Butterfield and head of product Merci Grace acting as co-Deciders. The two of them had several sketches from which to choose, each outlining a different approach to explaining Slack to new customers. Stewart's favorite was a proposal for a kind of "work game" that would let people test-drive Slack by talking to chatbots. Merci chose a simpler proposal: a "product tour" that detailed Slack's key features—and why they were better than email.

The Slack team proceeded to build two realistic prototypes: one for the work game, and one for the product tour. They gave each a different brand name, so that they appeared to be marketing websites for two completely different products. Then they tested the two with potential customers who had never heard of Slack.

People were confused by the chatbots. But Merci's choice, the product tour, got customers excited enough to sign up for a demo. Slack went on to build and launch a new marketing website based on that product tour, and it helped propel their record-breaking growth.

Because real products take so long, few teams can afford to build more than one at a time. In a Design Sprint, however, you can easily make and test multiple prototypes in parallel. This *Hunger Games*–style approach helps you make smarter decisions by exploring different solutions before you commit.*

Face the competition

When we run Design Sprints with startups in the Character portfolio, we also pit their prototypes against the top competition, whether that's another product, a substitute, or the status quo (see chapter 4).

*Another great example comes from Steve Jobs, who asked his teams at Apple to develop two competing prototypes for a smartphone: one with a click wheel, based on the original iPod, and another with a touch screen. Spoiler alert: the touch screen won.

Sometimes facing the competition is sobering: They might be stronger than you think. Sometimes it's encouraging: You might spot new opportunities. Every time, watching customers "shop" for the best choice adds a valuable dose of reality—and a big confidence boost once your solution clicks.

Repeat until it clicks

Every once in a while, a team creates the perfect solution in their first Design Sprint. More often, it goes as it did for Phaidra: You get a few things right, then you adjust and repeat. It's extremely common for teams to modify not just their solution but also their Founding Hypothesis during these early sprints. Teams change their target customer. They change their differentiators. They change their approach. JZ and I don't think of these adjustments as failures, but hyperefficient pivots.

Watch for reactions

How will you know when your solution finally clicks? If you want to remove all doubt, test whether customers will spend real time or money on your solution. Include a payment form in your prototype, or a scheduling form for setting up a sales demo.

But other signals can give you the confidence to stop sprinting and start building. In particular, as you test with customers, watch for the difference between *feedback* and *reactions*.

Feedback—that is, customers giving you advice about your solution, or telling you what they think you ought to do—is sometimes valuable. But reactions—that is, genuine unguarded moments when people respond to your product—are solid gold.

Salespeople are often masters at interpreting reactions and understanding a customer's state of mind. As you interview customers one-on-one in Design Sprints, you, too, will quickly become attuned to their physical and verbal signals. When customers lean forward, when they ask if they can start using your solution right away, when they try to pull it out of your hands—that's the good stuff. When it clicks, you'll know.

Some folks object to the one-on-one customer tests in Design Sprints. They argue that you won't know whether you have product-market fit until your *product* launches to the *market*.

This argument? It's not wrong. When you have a real product out in the real world and real people are spending real time and real money on it (or not), you can tell, for real, if you have product-market fit. If you test a prototype with individuals, that is just flat-out *not* the same thing. It's a simulation.

However, this kind of simulation is a powerful educational tool. I think about it like this: Would I rather ride with a pilot who's following a hunch about how to fly the aircraft—or one with lots of experience in a simulator? Given that choice, a simulator sounds pretty good to me.

Now, it is also true that individuals are not a substitute for the entire market. But then again, what *is* the market? It's not a farmers' market or a supermarket or a flea market. No, the "market" in "product-market fit" is business jargon for *a large group of people who have something in common, and to whom we can sell stuff.* This kind of market might be anything: people who work with remote teams, people who manufacture chemicals, people who hate email, people who love sandwiches, people who live in Milwaukee, you name it. The common element is *people.* A market is just a concept; what we're really talking about is a bunch of individuals.

While it's certainly true that the reaction of one individual won't predict what everyone in the market will do, it is a pretty darned interesting signal.

If you talk to five or ten or fifteen people in your market and your solution doesn't click with *any* of them, that's clearly bad news. If, on the other hand, your solution clicks with most or all of them? That's exciting. That, my friends, is a hell of a lot better than trusting a hunch for a year (or more) while you wait to get perfect data. Because in the end, it's simple: if a product clicks for enough people, that's product-market fit.

Congratulations, you made it to the end of the ten lessons, and now, whenever you see this book, you can say to yourself, "Hey, I read that!" That's a good feeling. But I hope this will be more than a book that you completed reading: I want it to help you get the most out of your future efforts. So, if you're up for it, stick with me for a few more pages, and I'll show you how all these lessons fit together so you can put them into action.

Afterword: The System

Running a venture fund, as I do with JZ and Eli, is *not* the career I dreamed of as a kid.

When I was a kid, I wanted to be like Doc Brown, the guy from *Back to the Future* with the terrific hair who turns his DeLorean into a time machine. I didn't want to be an investor—what's an investor? I wanted to be an *inventor*.

To tell the truth, I wasn't exactly sure what inventors did, but I imagined I'd combine gears and pulleys with household objects, in the style of Rube Goldberg, and somehow make a scientific breakthrough. I experimented with cardboard, twine, kabob skewers, and miles of Scotch tape. It was a lot of fun, although I did not manage to produce a working flux capacitor.

Physics and general relativity stood in the way of my grand ambitions, so I turned my attention to computers. I built my homemade video games, then websites, then software. I discovered how long ambitious projects take and how challenging it is to work with a team of people. I realized that the beginnings of these projects matter a lot, and that nobody had a recipe for doing it right, so I spent years on a quest for the perfect start.

Along the way, I discovered that what I actually like most—even more than inventing new products myself—is helping others unlock their best work.

No doubt, running a venture fund is not the same as being a wild-haired genius with a pocketful of plutonium. But every time I get the chance to help teams start a big project—projects that, for many of them, are their life's work—I feel like I'm at the chalkboard with Doc Brown.

My biggest DeLorean moments happen during Character Labs, when JZ, Eli, and I get the chance to work with brand-new founders. We invest in a group of folks with outstanding capabilities, insight, and motivation who are just forming their new companies. Then we work together with that group of startups for a full month.

For me, Character Labs is a total blast. It's the dream situation: world-class teams, ambitious projects at the moment of inception, and a calendar under my control.

In that dream situation, with the opportunity to apply everything we know and craft the perfect beginning, here's what we do: We start with a Foundation Sprint to help founders get to the heart of their project and form a hypothesis. Then we run consecutive Design Sprints so they can test that hypothesis.

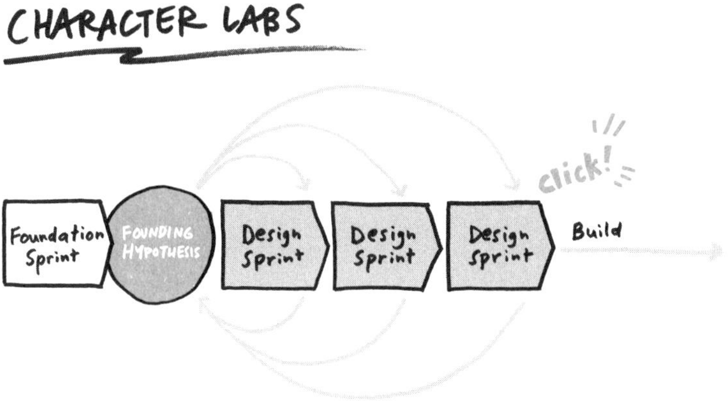

This system—a Foundation Sprint followed by consecutive Design Sprints—is powerful. Some founders see their solution click with customers in the first Design Sprint, and they refine from there. Some founders are still adjusting their differentiation at the end of the month. In any event, they radically increase their velocity and jump closer to making a product people want.

This is the system we use to give an unfair advantage to the startups in whom we invest. You can use the system, too. It's the perfect way to start a big project because it applies all of the ten key lessons from this book:

1. **Drop everything and sprint on the most important challenge until it's done.**
2. **Start by identifying your customer and a real problem you can solve.**

3. **Take advantage of your advantages.**
4. **Get real about the competition.**
5. **Differentiation makes products click.**
6. **Use practical principles to reinforce differentiation.**
7. **Seek alternatives to your first idea.**
8. **Consider conflicting opinions before you commit to an approach.**
9. **It's just a hypothesis until you prove it.**
10. **Experiment with tiny loops until your solution clicks. Then build it.**

We believe in these ten lessons because they're forged from our firsthand experience. Some of that experience comes from my time with Gmail and Google Meet and JZ's time working on Google Ads and YouTube. Some of that experience comes from founding Character Capital. But most of it comes from our time working alongside founders.

In our first book, *Sprint*, we shared the stories of startups including Blue Bottle Coffee, Flatiron Health, One Medical, and Slack. Each was intensely customer-focused, knew its own strengths, and was honest about its competition. Each developed strong differentiation, considered competing approaches, and ran multiple sprints to prototype and test solutions until they clicked.

When we wrote *Sprint*, all four were small startups, but in time, each grew into a valuable company. In 2017, Blue Bottle Coffee was acquired by Nestlé for $700M. In 2018, Flatiron Health was acquired by Roche for $1.9B. In 2020, One Medical went public, and was later acquired by Amazon for $3.9B. In 2019, Slack went public, and was later acquired by Salesforce for $28B. Many factors contributed to these successes. But in the early days, as they embarked on massive projects, these founders and teams embodied all ten lessons.

These lessons, however, are not just for startups. JZ and I have heard from people around the world who have applied these methods to all kinds of challenges.

A doctor named Camille Fleming used sprints to start her big project: opening a health care clinic in a rural community. She crafted a hypothesis, sketched solutions, prototyped a marketing website with Squarespace, and tested with locals. The first customers weren't interested. So she adjusted her hypothesis, updated her prototype, tried again—and this time, the clinic clicked. People wanted to sign up on the spot. Camille built the confidence to leave her old job and launch the business, and today she has a staff of three and so many customers she's had to set up a waiting list.

Sebastian Stricker, a former officer with the United Nations World Food Programme, used this method to start his big project: a "get one, give one" business that sells snacks, water, soap, clothing, and other items in Germany and, for each item sold, delivers food, water, and supplies to those in need. It took trial and error, but he and his team adjusted until they found packaging and a recipe that clicked with shoppers. Their flagship product, the "share bar," became a big hit in Germany and, as of this writing, the company has distributed over 56 million meals, over 21 million hygiene products, and over 86 million days' worth of clean drinking water.

In Brussels, Gaël Mercier brought these methods to the local public transportation agency. Many of the agency's hypotheses and experiments involve taking physical prototypes—new signs, station designs, and so forth—out on city streets to test with real commuters. (They even ran a Design Sprint to prevent people from cheating on their fares, and tested their prototype by interviewing . . . fare cheaters. Way to put the customer first!)

In Sweden, Helen Bjorkman and her team have run more than one hundred Design Sprints at the manufacturing giant Tetra Pak, prototyping and testing hypotheses for everything from onboarding new employees to streamlining factory repairs. In Argentina, Hernán Virgolini brought Design Sprints to secondary schools, setting up programs that teach students how to develop and test hypotheses. At Harvard Business School, Alan MacCormack and Russ Wilcox lead cohorts of MBA and engineering students through Design Sprints at the start of every winter term. In Denmark, LEGO handed out copies of our book *Sprint* to an entire division of workers, then spent eight weeks straight experimenting to develop new products. Today LEGO has run hundreds of Design Sprints on big projects spanning everything from marketing to factory operations to finance to human resources. The list goes on.

I asked our cofounder Eli Blee-Goldman what it is about working in this way that's so powerful. Eli spent many years as an investor before we started Character Capital, and in his career, he's invested in hundreds of startups and gotten to know thousands of founders. "The headline of these sprints is progress toward product-market fit," he told me. "But what's most amazing to me is how it builds trust and camaraderie within the team. Everyone sees each other's unique contributions. That psychological boost is real, and it lasts long after the sprints."

Eli's comments ring true with me. Many people who have tried our sprint methods tell me that it not only worked, it transformed their careers. They signed up for their jobs eager to make a difference in people's lives, only to find themselves mired in business as usual, ricocheting off competing priorities and office politics all day long. Then, when they cleared their calendars and ran sprints, they finally got the time and structure to do the work that matters most. They reconnected with the deeper purpose of their jobs and built a stronger bond with their colleagues. They unlocked their best work. In many cases, they tell me they felt like kids again. Like inventors!

You can do the same. Start with a Foundation Sprint. Put your customer at the center and define what you can do for them. Test this Founding Hypothesis in Design Sprints until your solution clicks. Then build it, launch it, and solve an important problem for real people.

There's just one thing: This new way of working requires a leader. Someone must introduce the Foundation Sprint to the team, build excitement, and make it happen—and you know who, having just finished reading this book, is perfectly qualified?

You.

When you're ready, the checklist awaits. I wish you speed on your journey, meaningful work along the way, and a solution that clicks.

Next steps

- Turn the page for the **Foundation Sprint Checklist**.
- Check out theclickbook.com for an **interactive guide with videos**.
- Check out our book *Sprint* and thesprintbook.com for more about **Design Sprints**.
- If you're building a startup, we'd love to hear from you! Visit character.vc to learn about **Character Capital**, get in touch, and apply for **Character Labs**.

The Foundation Sprint Checklist

The Foundation Sprint is a two-day workshop for a team at the beginning of a big project. On the morning of day one, you'll define the basics of your project, then, in the afternoon, you'll craft differentiation to help you stand out from the competition. On day two, you'll evaluate multiple options and choose an approach to your project. By the end, you'll have a Founding Hypothesis: a clear statement of what you believe that can be proved (or disproved) with Design Sprints.

GET READY

- [ ] **Check out our interactive guide**

  You can use the guide as a virtual whiteboard to run your Foundation Sprint. You'll find it on theclickbook.com.

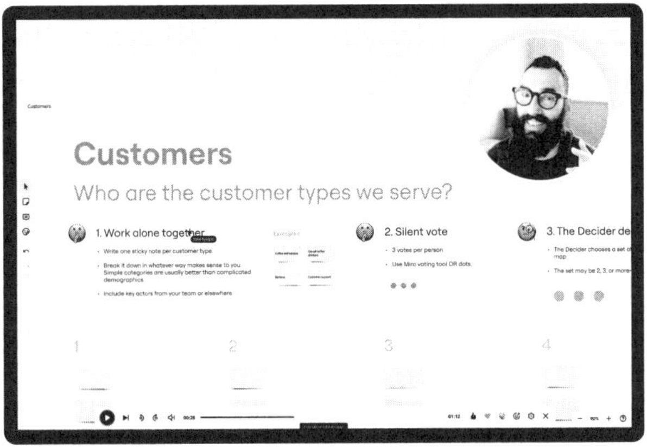

- [ ] **Start with the Decider**

  Get the real boss in the room so decisions stick. Once the Decider signs up, he or she can pave the way for assembling the rest of the team and clearing the schedule. (p. 30)

- [ ] **Form a tiny team**

  No more than five people, including the Decider. Look for folks with contrasting perspectives. (p. 31)

- [ ] **Choose a Facilitator**

  The Facilitator will guide the team through this checklist, so he or she should be comfortable leading a meeting. The Facilitator could be on the sprint team or an outsider. Since you're reading this, you're a great candidate.

- [ ] **Block two full days on the calendar**

  Six hours per day provides plenty of breathing room to finish the activities *and* take ample breaks. Our favorite time slot is 10 a.m. to 4 p.m. because it doesn't start too early or end too late.

❑ **Declare a good emergency**

Let others know you'll be offline. Try a variation of this message: "*Hey, our team is totally focused on (our most important project), so I have to cancel and I'll be slow to reply until it's done.*" (p. 31)

If your team will meet in person:

❑ **Book a room with a big whiteboard**

In the Foundation Sprint, the whiteboard becomes a shared brain for the team. The more whiteboard space you have, the bigger the brain. (Even if you plan to use the interactive template in person, a physical whiteboard will also be useful.)

❑ **Stock up on supplies**

Yellow sticky notes and black markers are best because they preserve anonymity and reduce cognitive load for the team. You should also get colorful sticky notes (only for the Magic Lenses activity), blank white paper, dot stickers for voting, and snacks. Find links to our favorite supplies on theclickbook.com.

❑ **Print a Foundation Sprint workbook for each person on the team**

You can find a PDF with fill-in-the-blank worksheets on theclickbook.com.

DAY 1

Note: Schedules are approximate. Don't worry if you run a little behind—the schedule ends 30 minutes early to give you some overflow time. Take breaks every 60 to 90 minutes.

10:00 a.m.—RESET

- ❑ **Introductions**
  Make sure everyone knows everyone. Introduce the Decider and explain their role. Explain that you will be guiding the process.
- ❑ **Give a tour of the Foundation Sprint**
  Even if everyone knows why you're sprinting, remind them. Give them a walk-through of the template.
- ❑ **Introduce "Get started not perfect"**
  The Foundation Sprint isn't about a perfect launch plan, but instead a clear hypothesis you can test right away. (p. 33)
- ❑ **Introduce "Work alone together"**
  Collaboration works differently in a Foundation Sprint. Feel free to quote us: "*Jake and JZ say that it might be awkward, but it's an effective way to compress time, get everyone involved, and make quick decisions.*" (p. 32)

10:30-ish—BASICS

- ❑ **Choose your target customer (about 15 minutes)**
  Use plain language. Simple categories are better than complicated demographics. (p. 39) Work alone together using a Note-and-Vote:

  1. Everyone takes five minutes to think in silence. Each person writes one or more answers, each on a separate sticky note. Keep answers anonymous.
  2. Put the sticky notes up where everyone can see.

CHECKLIST

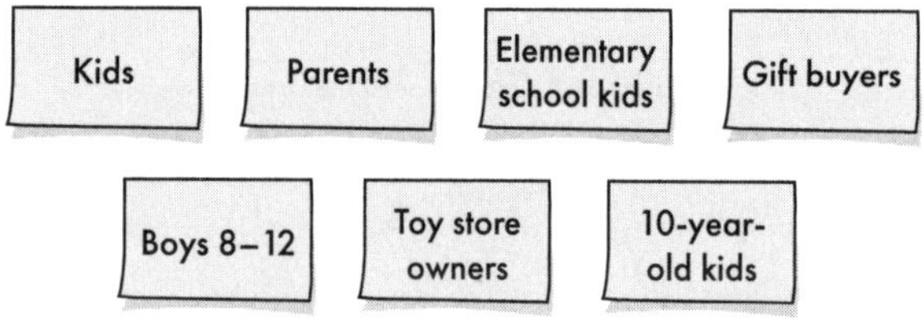

3. Each person reviews in silence for about five minutes and places two or three votes for their favorite proposals.

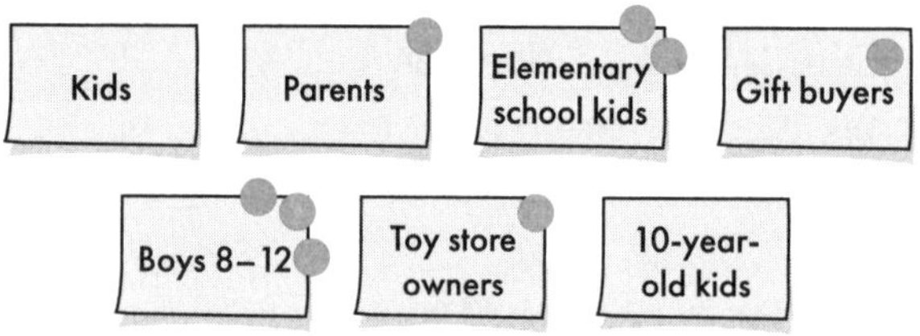

4. The Decider may call for a short debate about his or her top options.
5. The Decider chooses one option.

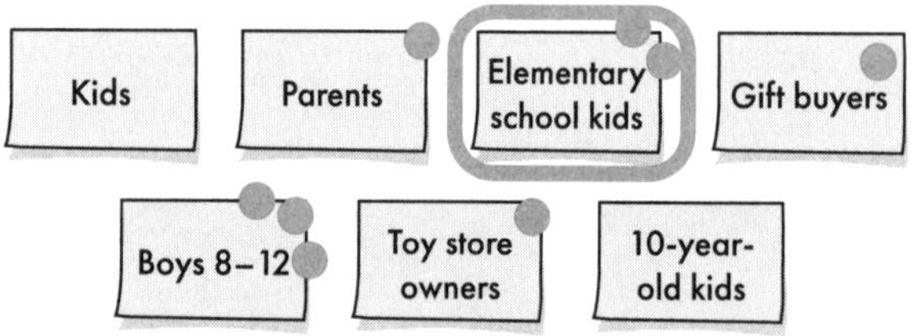

- ❑ **Choose your target customer problem (about 15 minutes)**
  Note-and-Vote. The Decider chooses one problem statement. (p. 43)
- ❑ **Identify your advantages (about 15 minutes)**
  Note-and-Vote. Identify the capabilities, insights, and motivations that make your team uniquely suited to solve this problem. The Decider chooses three advantages—one of each type. (p. 60)
- ❑ **List your competitors (about 15 minutes)**
  Note-and-Vote. Consider direct competitors, substitutes, and "do nothing." The Decider chooses three to five competitors—as well as the one most important "eight-hundred-pound gorilla." (p. 69)
- ❑ **Fill out the Basics**
  Put your customer, problem, advantages, and competition on one page.

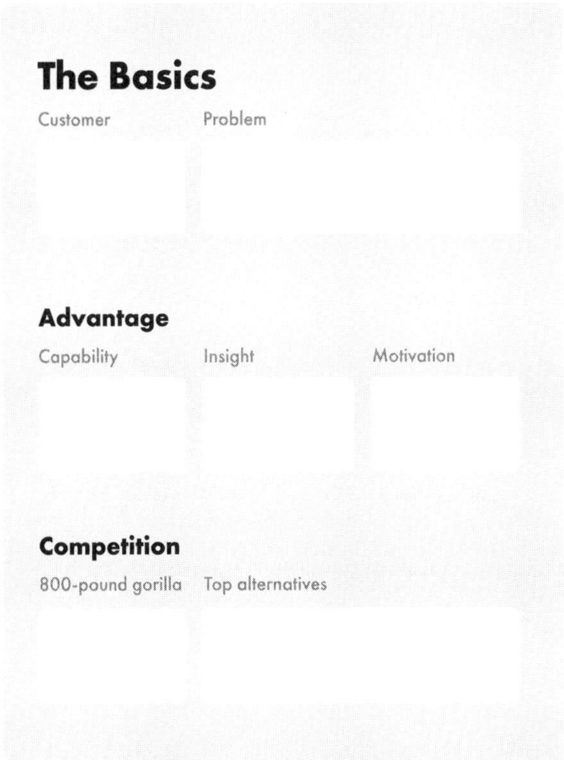

11:30 a.m.

- ❑ **Take a break (about 30 minutes)**
  Get a snack or lunch. Stand up and stretch or take a walk.

12:00 p.m.—DIFFERENTIATION

- ❑ **Differentiation classics (about 20 minutes)**
  Use realistic optimism. Mark where your solution *could* stack up against the competition. Work alone together. (p. 90)

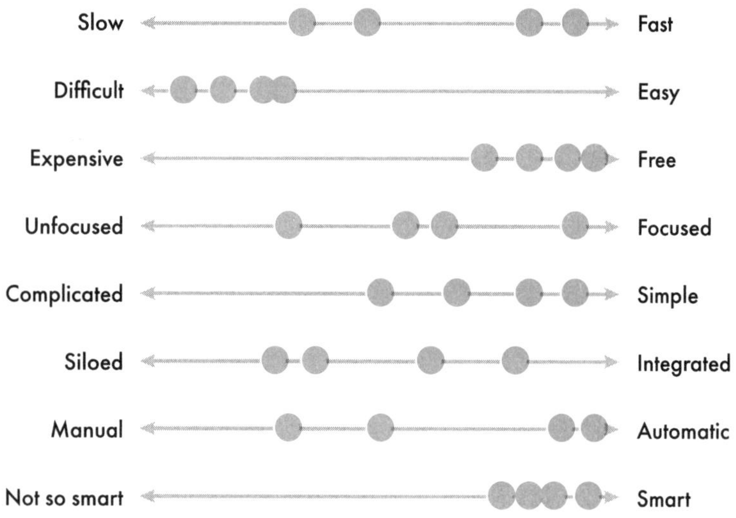

- ❑ **Choose your own differentiators (about 20 minutes)**
  Stay in realistic optimism mode. Generate your own scales, using criteria at which your solution could excel—and which would make the competition look crummy. Work alone together. (p. 90)

- ❑ **Score your differentiators, part 2 (about 10 minutes)**
  Review the custom differentiators. Once again, mark where your solution could stack up against the competition.
- ❑ **Choose differentiators (about 5 minutes)**
  Everyone votes silently on their top six differentiators (you can vote on both the classic and custom spectrums). The Decider chooses the top two differentiators to try first—although you'll probably have to try several in the next step before you get it right.

1:00 p.m.

- ❑ **Take a break (about 60 minutes)**
  Get a snack or lunch. Stand up and stretch or take a walk.

2:00 p.m.

- ❑ **Make a 2x2 differentiation chart (about 45 minutes)**
  Focus on customer perception, not technology. Experiment with differentiators until you find two that give you lots of space. Don't settle for mediocre differentiation—push the competition into Loserville. But be honest. Differentiation only works if you can deliver what you promise. (p. 93)

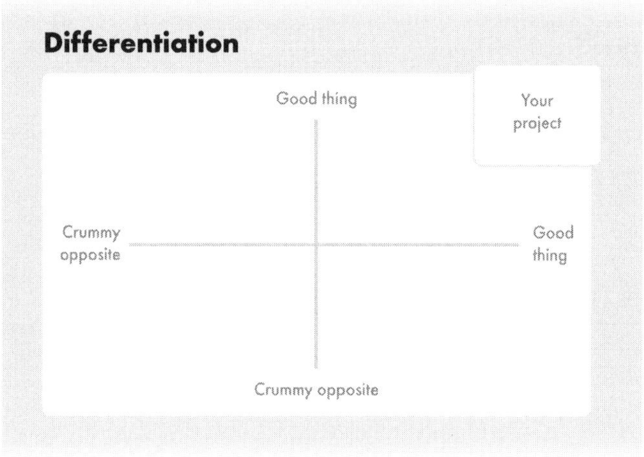

2:45-ish

- ❑ **Draft practical principles (about 45 minutes)**
  Note-and-Vote. Be practical. Consider differentiation ("What advice would I give a new team member to make sure we follow through on our differentiation?") and safeguards ("How can we protect against success that harms our customers?"). The Decider chooses three-ish principles. (p. 106)
- ❑ **Fill out the Mini Manifesto**
  Put your 2x2 and principles in one place. (p. 107)

3:30 p.m.

- ❑ **Call it a day**

Mini Manifesto

Differentiation

Principles

1

2

3

DAY 2

10:00 a.m.—APPROACH

❑ **List all possible approaches (about 30 minutes)**

Note-and-Vote. Generate multiple alternate approaches to the project. Start with known options. Imagine your first choice fails—what would you do then? Consider alternate customers, too. The Decider chooses three to seven options. (p. 123)

- [ ] **Make a one-page summary for each approach (about 30 minutes)**
Divide the approaches. Work alone together. Include a summary (reference the problem and differentiation) and a doodle showing how it might work. (p. 124)

Approach summary

What it is (write the title of this approach)

Why it's a good idea (write one sentence)

How it might work (draw a quick doodle)

11:00 a.m.

- [ ] **Take a break (about 30 minutes)**
Get a snack or lunch.

11:30 a.m.—MAGIC LENSES

- ❑ **Assign a color to each approach (about 10 minutes)**
  Gather the one-page summaries. Assign each a letter or a color (or both). This will make it easier to spot patterns later.

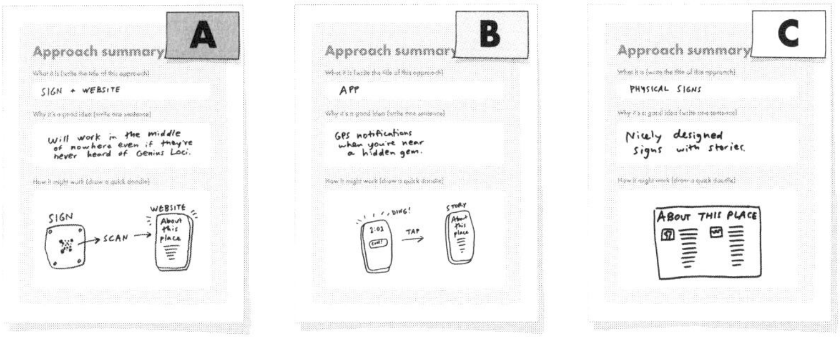

- ❑ **List criteria for each approach (about 20 minutes)**
  Work alone together. Read the summaries in silence. Label each approach with its positive criteria. (For example, if it's easy to build, label it "Easy to build." If it has a large potential audience, label it "Large potential audience." And so on.) Aim for one to four criteria per approach.

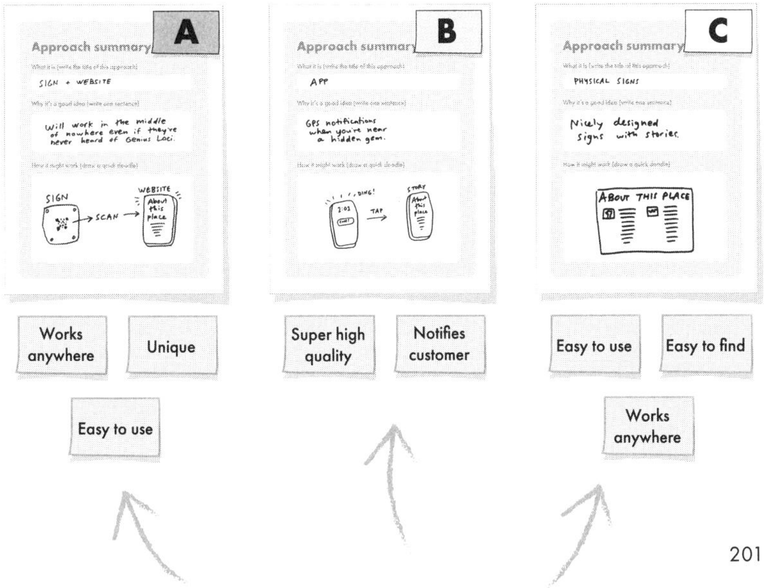

CHECKLIST

❑ **Make "team of rivals" charts (about 15 minutes)**

Create the four default charts: customer lens, pragmatic lens, growth lens, and money lens. The default labels ("Easy to use" to "Hard to use," etc.) are just a starting point. Most teams customize the labels to make it fit what matters to their project. (p. 134)

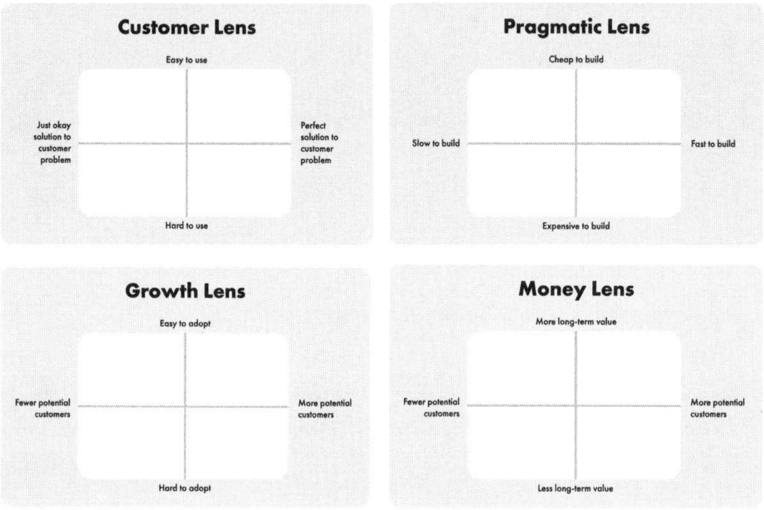

❑ **Place your options on each chart (about 45 minutes)**

JZ and I find it easiest to plot one axis at a time, asking an expert on the team or the Decider to help with relative placement. "*Where does this go? Higher or lower than this one? Sounds like more of a six than a five?*" Feel free to adjust the criteria on the charts as you go—the default labels above are just a starting point.

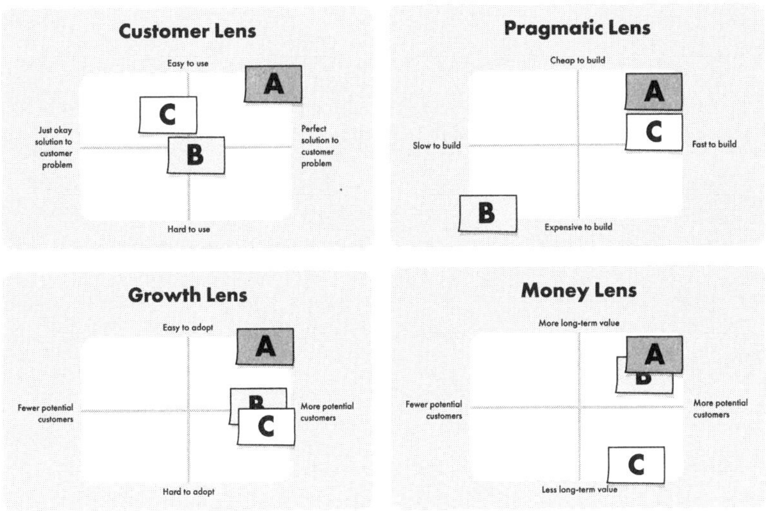

1:00 p.m.

- ❑ **Take a break (about 60 minutes)**
  Get a snack or lunch.

2:00 p.m.

- ❑ **Review the criteria (about 5 minutes)**
  In silence, review the criteria and add more. Vote on the most important ones for making the product click. The Decider chooses two.
- ❑ **Make custom 2x2 charts (about 30 minutes)**
  Start with the Decider's criteria. Plot the approaches. Adjust criteria and the placement of your options until the chart seems right. Give this new chart a name. Repeat. Aim for two to four additional charts. (p. 131)
- ❑ **Try your differentiation 2x2 chart (about 10 minutes)**
  Plot the approaches on your differentiation chart from day one.

2:45-ish

- ❑ **Zoom out and review (about 10 minutes)**
  Stand back or zoom out in your whiteboard software. Look for patterns. Does one approach win every time? Does one 2x2 strike you as the most useful lens? Does one or more contradict the others? (p. 139)
- ❑ **The Decider decides (about 5 minutes)**
  Choose one top bet (your first choice approach for the project) and one backup plan (the next approach to consider if you need to pivot).

3:15-ish

- ❑ **Fill out the Founding Hypothesis (about 15 minutes)**
  Put every key decision from the Foundation Sprint in one place.

3:30 p.m.

- ❑ **Your Foundation Sprint is complete!**
  Take a break—you've earned it—and then get ready to test your hypothesis.

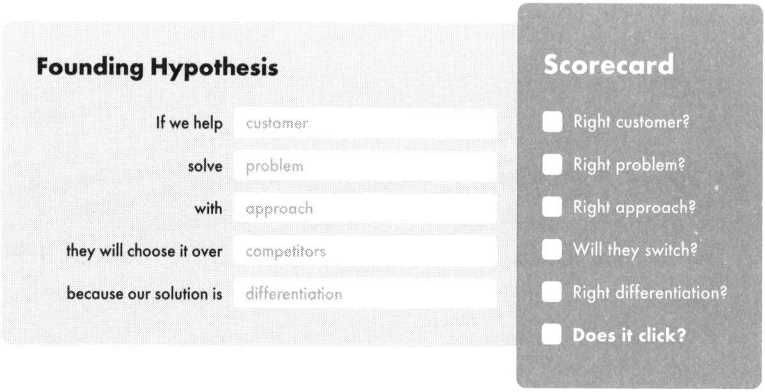
Founding Hypothesis
If we help
customer
solve
problem
with
approach
they will choose it over
competitors
because our solution is
differentiation
Scorecard
Right customer?
Right problem?
Right approach?
Will they switch?
Right differentiation?
Does it click?

FAQ

Q: Is the Foundation Sprint only for startups?

A: No.

We designed the Foundation Sprint for startups, but organizations of all sizes and kinds can benefit from the same structure at the beginning of big projects.

Q: Our project is already underway. Is it too late for a Foundation Sprint?

A: No.

If your team is stuck in endless debate or unsure whether customers will care about what you're building, it's better to call a time-out and run a Foundation Sprint than to keep running in what might be the wrong direction.

Q: Can we run a Foundation Sprint on its own, without Design Sprints?

A: Yes.

The Foundation Sprint is a great start for any big project. If you don't run Design Sprints afterward, you'll have to find another way to test your Founding Hypothesis. Just don't wait too long.

Q: Can we compress the Foundation Sprint into one day?

A: Yes, if you're willing to do homework.

If you do the Basics beforehand (either in a separate meeting, or as asynchronous homework), it's possible to squeeze Differentiation and Approach into one day.

Q: Should I modify the Foundation Sprint?

A: No, not the first time you try it.

We've optimized the steps of the Foundation Sprint based on our experience running sprints with hundreds of teams. We recommend you try our way at least once (and maybe two or three times) before you alter it. Once you've got a good feel for the original recipe, feel free to experiment—and if you find new techniques that work well, please let us know!

Q: Can I use parts of the Foundation Sprint without running the whole process?

A: Yes, but be careful.

If you're already committed to an approach, you can run a Differentiation Sprint (just the first day of a Foundation Sprint). You can also run an Opportunity Sprint (just the second day of a Foundation Sprint) to help make any kind of big, complex decision. But be careful, because the two days are designed to work together: it's best to choose an approach for your project that is informed by your differentiation.

Q: The Decider can't join. Will the Foundation Sprint still work?

A: No.

Without the Decider, the decisions made in the Foundation

Sprint—and there are a *lot* of very important decisions!—simply won't stick. It's not good enough to have someone who is very familiar with the Decider's thinking. You need the actual Decider, so wait until she or he is available. If the Decider won't make time for the Foundation Sprint, the project probably isn't very important.

Q: Does the Decider have to be the CEO?

A: Not necessarily.

The Decider is the person with decision-making responsibility for the project. In early-stage startups, this is typically the CEO or another cofounder. In larger organizations, it's just the leader who makes decisions about the project.

Q: I'm not the Decider. How can I convince him or her to try a Foundation Sprint?

A: Tell the truth.

Sit down with the Decider and tell her or him why you think your team could benefit from a Foundation Sprint. Be honest. If you want to run a Foundation Sprint because your team is struggling to make decisions, lacks clarity about the fundamentals, or is moving too slow, then say that. If you want to run a Foundation Sprint simply because you're at the beginning of an ambitious project and you want to do everything possible to make it a winner for customers, then say that. Encourage the Decider to think of your first Foundation Sprint as an experiment, rather than a permanent change. And bring a copy of this book. It might sound weird, but even in our digital world, a physical book goes a long way toward giving new ideas credibility.

Q: The Decider doesn't want to try a Foundation Sprint. Should I give up?

A: No.

Don't stop working to make things better. Try introducing the Note-and-Vote in meetings. Try Magic Lenses for bigger decisions. You can also try breaking the Foundation Sprint into smaller pieces (see page 206) or run it by yourself (see below).

Q: Can I run a Foundation Sprint by myself?

A: Yes, but it's better with a team.

The Foundation Sprint can work as an individual exercise, but it's better with a team of people who can bring different perspectives—and, importantly, who will be invested in testing the Founding Hypothesis after the sprint is complete.

Q: Can our team run a Foundation Sprint even if we can't get together in the same place?

A: Absolutely.

Most of the Foundation Sprints we've run have been over video. It works great. Just use our interactive template on theclickbook.com.

Q: I'm a startup founder. Can I get in touch with Character Capital?

A: Yes!

We'd love to learn about you and the customer problem you're solving. Please visit character.vc—you can contact us there!

Thank-You Notes

This book would be no more than a pile of sticky notes without:

- Sylvie Carr, our agent, who guided *Click* all the way from half-baked idea to finished product. Sylvie, thanks for your patience, conviction, and leadership.
- Ben Loehnen, our editor at Avid Reader Press, who once again inspired us with high standards, sage advice, and timely encouragement. Ben, thanks for your enthusiasm and vision.
- The excellent team at Avid Reader Press and Simon & Schuster, including Carolyn Kelly, Ruth Lee-Mui, Samantha Hoback, Allison Green, Alison Forner, Sydney Newman, Clay Smith, Meredith Vilarello, Rhina Garcia, Emily Lewis, and Carolyn Levin, as well as copy editor Tom Pitoniak. Thanks for lending your talents to *Click* and being so gracious with our endless questions.
- Dan Heath, whose mentorship shaped this book. Dan, thanks for your insight and generosity.

- Jonathan Courtney, Laura Faint, Tim Höfer, Ryan de Metz, and the entire team at AJ&Smart who worked tirelessly to get *Click* into readers' hands. Jonathan and Laura, thanks for your energy and ingenuity.
- Lucy Oates, our editor at Penguin/Transworld in the UK, who time and again helped me see the text from a fresh perspective.
- Peter Griffin, whose editorial work sharpened, streamlined, and strengthened every chapter.
- Jessica Hische, who once again designed a cover that was not only everything I hoped it would be but also way better than I could imagine.
- Marin Licina, Ryan Brown, Erik Skogsberg, Blair Kreuzer, Xander Pollock, Jackie Colburn, Douglas Ferguson, Scott Rocher, Merci Grace, Henrik Bay, Eik Thyrsted Brandsgård, Katie Hoffman, Stéph Cruchon, and Eglé Cruchon, who provided useful and often blunt feedback on early drafts, changing the direction of the book much for the better. Thanks for your insight and honesty.

I'd also like to thank:

- John Zeratsky, whose wisdom is on every page. JZ, thanks for being my coconspirator once again.
- Eli Blee-Goldman, who brought countless insights to the Foundation Sprint and this book. Eli, thanks for your enduring confidence in this project.
- Irene Au, former head of design at Google, whose support made my first Design Sprint experiments possible and opened the path that eventually led to *Click*.
- Braden Kowitz, Daniel Burka, and Michael Margolis, our

colleagues at Google Ventures who helped us shape the Design Sprint and write *Sprint*.

- Blake Beale, Jim Wiggington, and Chelsie Lee, who gave me a great place to write.
- Everyone in Eastsound who unknowingly lifted my spirits on writing breaks, including Jenny, Kelly, Becky, Lisa, Erin, and the team at Darvill's Bookstore (the book jacket is red on their advice!); David, Lee, Caitlin, and the team at Brown Bear Baking; Linda, Sylvia, Ailia, Sara, and the team at Orcas Co-op; Jacob, Jason, and the team at Island Market; Sabrina, Spencer, and Quinn at Lone Pine Larder; and Andi, Anie, Claudia, and Bony at West Side Kitchen. Thank you for all the coffees, sandwiches, cookies, and friendly conversations.
- My mom, who listened to me read the entire book aloud (including many retakes) so I could get the words right. Mom, thanks for inspiring me to write in the first place.
- Becky, Roger, and Myla, who kept things running when the wheels nearly fell off.
- Flynn, whose keen design eye influenced many of *Click*'s illustrations, and Luke, who didn't give up on taking my author photo, even when I ruined an entire session with food in my beard.
- And Holly, who was the first and last editor, who always saw precisely what mattered and what did not, and who never gave up. Holly, without your support this book simply would not exist, and you gave it wholeheartedly even when it came at great cost. Thank you.

JZ would like to thank:

- Michelle Zeratsky, whose support, savvy, and love make everything better.

- Jake Knapp, the ideal collaborator, bringing wisdom, passion, and empathy to every project. Thanks for another fun one!
- Eli Blee-Goldman, who blends integrity, intelligence, and instinct in the daily work of building a new kind of venture capital firm. Thank you for trusting me!
- The dozens of investors, allocators, and friends who believed in us and backed their belief with capital.
- The team at Google Ventures, who provided a once-in-a-lifetime job that transformed my work life.
- Dozens of teams at YouTube and Google, who showed me what excellence looks like at scale.
- Matt Shobe, Dick Costolo, and the entire FeedBurner team, who empowered me to begin my career in the realest way possible.
- My parents, who gave me the confidence and freedom to see that anything was possible.

A very big thank-you to the founders and teams who welcomed us into their work and took a chance on our experiments—and to YOU, dear reader, for picking up this book and seeing it through. You're who we had in mind across the years, so thanks for being here in the end.

Image Credits

Stéph Cruchon took the photo on page 120.
Katie Hoffman took the photo of Jim Gao on page 163.
John Zeratsky took the photo of himself on page 163. (Nice selfie, JZ!)
Sketches and screenshots on pages 164, 165, and 167 courtesy of Phaidra.
All other illustrations by Jake Knapp.

Index

About the Authors

JAKE KNAPP is cofounder and general partner at Character Capital and a *New York Times* bestselling author. Previously, he helped build Gmail and Microsoft Encarta, cofounded Google Meet, and was a partner at Google Ventures. He lives on Orcas Island in Washington state.

JOHN ZERATSKY is cofounder and general partner at Character Capital and a *New York Times* bestselling author. Previously, JZ was a design leader for YouTube, Google Ads, and FeedBurner, a startup which was acquired by Google in 2007, and was a partner at Google Ventures. He lives in Milwaukee, Wisconsin.

Together, Jake and JZ are the authors of *Sprint*, *Make Time*, and *Click* and the creators of the Foundation Sprint and the Design Sprint. They have helped more than 300 teams design new products and bring them to market, including those at Google, Microsoft, YouTube, Slack, Uber, and One Medical Group. Their methods for innovation and rapid collaboration have been adopted by Airbnb, Amazon, LEGO, MIT, Mercedes-Benz, Harvard Business School, the University of Oxford, and many other organizations.